Buddhists, Hindus, and Sikhs in America

Religion in American Life

JON BUTLER & HARRY S. STOUT
GENERAL EDITORS

Buddhists, Hindus, and Sikhs in America

Gurinder Singh Mann,
Paul David Numrich &
Raymond B. Williams

OXFORD
UNIVERSITY PRESS

OXFORD
UNIVERSITY PRESS

Oxford New York
Athens Auckland Bangkok Bogotá Buenos Aires Cape Town
Chennai Dar es Salaam Delhi Florence Hong Kong Istanbul Karachi
Kolkata Kuala Lumpur Madrid Melbourne Mexico City Mumbai Nairobi
Paris São Paulo Singapore Taipei Tokyo Toronto Warsaw

and associated companies in
Berlin Ibadan

Copyright © 2001 by Gurinder Singh Mann,
Paul David Numrich, and Raymond Brady Williams

Published by Oxford University Press, Inc.
198 Madison Avenue, New York, New York 10016
www.oup.com

Oxford is a registered trademark of Oxford University Press

Library of Congress Cataloging-in-Publication Data
Mann, Gurinder Singh.
    Buddhists, Hindus, and Sikhs in America / Gurinder Singh Mann, Paul David Numrich &
Raymond Brady Williams.
        p. cm. – (Religion in American life)
    Includes bibliographical references and index.
    Summary: Presents the basic tenets of these three Asian religions and discusses the
religious history and experience of their practitioners after immigration to the United States.
    ISBN 0-19-512442-1
        1. Asian Americans—Religions—Juvenile literature. 2. Immigrants—Religious
life—United States—Juvenile literature. 3. United States—Emigration and immigration—
Religious aspects—Juvenile literature. 4. Buddhism—United States—History—20th
century—Juvenile literature. 5. Hinduism—United States—History—20th century—
Juvenile literature. 6. Sikhism—United States—History—20th century—Juvenile literature.
[1. Asian Americans—Religion. 2. Immigrants—Religious life. 3. Buddhism. 4. Hinduism.
5. Sikhism.] I. Numrich, Paul David, 1952- II. Williams, Raymond. III. Title. IV. Series.
BL2525.M356 2001
294'.0973—dc21   2001045151

9 8 7 6 5 4 3 2 1

Printed in the United States of America
on acid-free paper

Design: Loraine Machlin
Layout: Natalia Lytwakiwsky
. Picture research: Pat Burns and Jennifer Smith

On the cover: Plan for the Iraivan Temple, a Hindu temple designed for a site on the island of Kauai in Hawaii.

Frontispiece: Sikh Day Parade, April 1990, Madison Square Park, New York City.

Contents

Editors' Introduction

JON BUTLER & HARRY S. STOUT, GENERAL EDITORS

Buddhism, Hinduism, and Sikhism constitute three of the world's most powerful and intriguing religions. And the presence of Buddhists, Hindus, and Sikhs in the United States since the middle and late 19th century—and their dramatically increasing numbers since the 1960s—reveals the breadth of America's long-standing religious pluralism. The people of these faiths have faced and surmounted legal and social discrimination, and all three religions have survived and prospered in America among both Asian immigrants and their descendants and growing numbers of non-Asian converts.

Buddhists, Hindus, and Sikhs in America reveals the fascinating historical background of these vital religious traditions and outlines their encounter with America in the 19th and 20th centuries. Paul Numrich describes American intellectuals' fascination with Buddhism beginning in the 1840s and traces discrimination against Buddhism from anti-Chinese legislation in the 19th century to Japanese-American incarceration during World War II. Raymond Williams portrays Swami Vivekananda's impact at the 1893 Chicago World's Fair and Hinduism's remarkable adaptability and spiritual resilience in the 20th century to both Asian immigrants and American converts. Gurinder Singh Mann depicts how Sikh *gurdwaras,* or places of worship, have sustained core Sikh religious practices while accommodating American customs at the periphery—for example, sharing the traditional communal meal, but doing so in chairs instead of on

Brahmin priests pour water and place flowers on a tower to complete the dedication of a new Hindu temple. The tower rises directly above the image of the main deity inside the temple.

the floor as in India. Throughout, *Buddhists, Hindus, and Sikhs in America* explains how three of Asia's old world religions have prospered in the United States, and how they have refreshed America's dynamic religious pluralism through a presence as striking theologically as it is visually.

This book is part of a unique 17-volume series that explores the evolution, character, and dynamics of religion in American life from 1500 to the end of the 20th century. As late as the 1960s, historians paid relatively little attention to religion beyond studies of New England's Puritans. But since then, American religious history and its contemporary expression have been the subject of intense inquiry. These new studies have thoroughly transformed our knowledge of almost every American religious group and have fully revised our understanding of religion's role in U.S. history.

It is impossible to capture the flavor and character of the American experience without understanding the connections between secular activities and religion. Spirituality stood at the center of Native American societies before European colonization and has continued to do so long after. Religion—and the freedom to express it—motivated millions of immigrants to come to the United States from remarkably different cultures, and the exposure to new ideas and ways of living shaped their experience. It also fueled tension among different ethnic and racial groups in America and, regretfully, accounted for difficult episodes of bigotry in American society. Religion urged Americans to expand the nation—first within the continental United States, then through overseas conquests and missionary work—and has had a profound influence on American politics, from the era of the Puritans to the present. Finally, religion contributes to the extraordinary diversity that has, for four centuries, made the United States one of the world's most dynamic societies. The Religion in American Life series explores the historical traditions that have made religious freedom and spiritual exploration central features of American society. It emphasizes the experience of religion in America—what men and women have understood by religion, how it has affected politics and society, and how Americans have used it to shape their daily lives.

Religion in American Life

JON BUTLER & HARRY S. STOUT
GENERAL EDITORS

Introduction

PAUL DAVID NUMRICH

The religions featured in this book have all been transplanted to the United States from homelands in Asia. As in botany, transplantation does not mean exact duplication; it involves transformation. Plants grow differently in a new soil and climate. For example, I was once served Thai pumpkin at a Thai Buddhist temple in Chicago; when I asked my host whether Thai pumpkins grown in America taste the same as those grown in Thailand, he did not hesitate to answer, "No!" Like plants raised in other soil, then transplanted to a new environment, Buddhism, Hinduism, and Sikhism are evolving in new ways in America's cultural environment. They are being Americanized in ways welcomed by some people within the religions but lamented by others. Change is inevitable.

Hinduism originated in India so long ago that historians cannot determine its birth date. Buddhism began in the same region about 2,500 years ago and spread throughout Asia. Sikhism was born in the Punjab area of northwestern India around the late 1400s when Columbus was sailing to the Americas. Well established in their native countries, Buddhism, Hinduism, and Sikhism face similar questions as immigrant religions in the United States. For example, how can Buddhists, Hindus, and Sikhs preserve their traditions in this new situation?

Regardless of our religion, native ways are meaningful and comfort-

These Laotian-American boys are taking temporary ordination as Buddhist monks in a Des Moines, Iowa, temple. This traditional Theravada Buddhist practice teaches the beliefs and ideal practices of the faith, such as wisdom, compassion, and self-discipline.

ing, and integral to who we are. But immigrants begin to understand themselves in unexpected and unfamiliar ways in their new country. They discover that they must adapt to different realities, and it is not always clear what they should preserve as essential and what must change with the times. For many Buddhist, Hindu, and Sikh immigrants in America, the tension between wanting to preserve their original culture and needing to innovate plays out through their religious beliefs and practices, at home and religious centers.

In a new country, questions about fundamental beliefs and age-old practices begin to arise. When a religion develops as an integral part of the culture of a specific country or region, its followers may equate their religion with the larger culture. They may assume that their particular forms of cultural expression represent the entire religion. But when they emigrate they meet fellow believers from other cultures who understand and express the same religion differently. Buddhists from Thailand discover Buddhists from Japan, for instance, and Hindus from one region in India may become neighbors to Hindus from other regions. Asian Buddhists, Hindus, and Sikhs have even found non-Asian Americans practicing their religions here, from conversion rather than birth. Such discoveries often lead immigrants to reexamine their native religious traditions, to ask what aspects of Buddhism are shared by all Buddhists, what tenets of Hinduism are common among all Hindu groups, what is the core of Sikhism that applies to Punjabi and non-Punjabi Sikhs alike. The new religious understandings and practices that emerge from these encounters are part of becoming American.

Another shared concern has to do with the second and later generations, the descendants of the immigrants who first settled in the United States. Buddhist, Hindu, and Sikh parents typically wishing to transfer their native heritage to their offspring educate them about the history, culture, language, values, and religion of their homeland. They take their children to the local Buddhist or Hindu temple or Sikh *gurdwara*, send them to summer camps or to visit relatives in the original country, and work to instill in them an appreciation of their ethnic roots and identity. Tensions often arise between the two generations, though, because they come from different worlds: the parents born in one culture, the children in another. The later generations are frequently more American than their parents usually want, the immigrant generation still more traditional than their children can appreciate. Every immigrant generation fears that its offspring will forget their past. Every later generation wishes its parents could understand what it means to be born an American.

Buddhist, Hindu, and Sikh immigrants also share something that has significantly affected their new life in America. Both racially and religiously they differ from the larger population of the United States. All three groups are part of Asian America, considered by many other Americans to be "strangers from a different shore," as the Japanese-American historian Ronald Takaki terms them. They came to America for the opportunities and promises it offered, but they were often unwelcomed by the Americans already here. The prejudice and discrimination that Asian Americans have endured over the years is summed up in U.S. immigration law, which restricted the entrance of Asians for much of our history. The majority of America's Buddhists, Hindus, and Sikhs are here today as a result of relaxed changes in immigration law in 1965, either as new immigrants or offspring of new immigrants.

American society can be likened to a garden with many plants. Various ethnic and immigrant groups practicing many different religious traditions make the United States a complex multicultural society. As in a garden with many plants, the range of characteristics makes the American garden all the more interesting.

Chapter 1

Buddhism Comes to America

Three religions stand out today as truly global in scope, with hundreds of millions of followers from many nationalities and ethnic groups. The majority of Americans belong to the largest of these three world religions, Christianity. Americans typically know something about the second largest of the three, Islam, however shaped their knowledge may be by the often strained relations between the Western world and the Middle East, Islam's birthplace. The third truly global religion, Buddhism, presents a more complex puzzle to Americans.

Buddhism's founder, Siddhartha Gautama, was born a prince in a small kingdom in what is now Nepal, on India's northern border, around 500 B.C.E. Despite his fortunate circumstances, Siddhartha came to see life as basically unsatisfying. The suffering caused by old age, disease, and death particularly troubled him, so at the age of 29 he began a search for peace of mind or liberation from the dissatisfactions of human experience. Six years later he attained his goal, proclaiming to have discovered an ultimate consciousness called Nirvana, or enlightenment, that rises above or transcends ordinary human states of mind. After this time Siddhartha was known as the Buddha, meaning "Enlightened One."

In his first sermon after enlightenment, the Buddha preached the Four Noble Truths of Buddhism: that life is unsatisfactory, that it is our

A Buddhist priest poses with some members of the Oakland Buddhist Church in California in 1914. Like most of the early Japanese *bukkyokai* (Buddhist associations or temples) in the United States, the Oakland temple probably adopted the mainstream American term "church" in response to anti-Japanese sentiment.

Malunkya's Questions

In a Buddhist scripture called "The Lesser Discourse to Malunkya," the Buddha teaches his disciple Malunkya a lesson about living a religious life. Malunkya was troubled that his Master had not answered certain important questions in his mind, for instance: Did the universe have a beginning and will it end someday, or has the universe always existed and will there never be an end to it? What happens to enlightened people after they die? Malunkya was prepared to leave the Buddha's path unless he received some answers. Rather than answering his disciple's questions directly, the Buddha instead redirected Malunkya's attention to the more important topic of living a religious life.

"It is not on the view that the world [the universe] is eternal . . . that a religious life depends," said the Buddha regarding one of his disciple's questions. "Whether the view is held that the world is eternal, or that the world is not eternal, there is still rebirth [multiple lifetimes], there is old age, there is death, and grief, lamentation, suffering, sorrow, and despair, the destruction of which even in this life I announce."

Using an analogy, the Buddha likened Malunkya's useless concerns to [those of] a man wounded by a poisoned arrow who refused treatment until he knew his attacker's name, what type of person he was, how tall, what race, his hometown, and what kind of bow and arrow he had used—all the while the man lay dying.

desires that cause life's unsatisfactoriness, that Nirvana is liberation from life's unsatisfactoriness, and that there is a path leading to Nirvana. Notably absent from the Buddha's teachings were two notions commonly found in Western religions: the existence of an eternal, individual human soul and the existence of an eternal, unchanging, almighty God who created the universe. (Buddhists do believe in spiritual beings or deities, but not in this sense.) The Buddha taught his spiritual path to others for many years, modeling in his own life the key Buddhist virtues of wisdom and compassion until he passed away at the age of 80.

In the centuries after the Buddha's life, Buddhism spread throughout Asia. The great third-century B.C.E. Indian emperor Asoka apparently favored Buddhism. Tradition says that he sent Buddhist missionaries to Ceylon, now known as Sri Lanka, and to Southeast Asia, areas that became the geographic heart of one major branch of Buddhism called Theravada, which means the Way (or Tradition) of the Elders. Another major branch, Mahayana (the "Large Vehicle," or movement), took hold in northeastern Asia. Mahayana Buddhism includes more diversity of thought and practice than Theravada. Several versions, or schools, of Mahayana arose in China and Japan. Among these were the Pure Land, Zen, and Nichiren groups. A third major branch of Buddhism, called Vajrayana—which means "Thunderbolt (or Diamond) Vehicle," a reference to its purported power—is centered mainly in Tibet. The Dalai Lama, one of the world's most widely recognized religious figures, heads one school of Tibetan Buddhism.

Religious practices vary among the many branches and schools of Buddhism, and local expressions of Buddhism draw from the unique cultures of different areas. All Buddhists, however, share a deep reverence for the Buddha as their religious teacher and guide. Buddhists often repeat this basic statement about seeking spiritual "refuge" or security in life: "I take refuge in the Buddha, I take refuge in the Dharma [the Buddha's teachings], I take refuge in the Sangha [the Buddha's disciplined followers]."

Beginning around 1500, several Western powers entered Buddhist areas of Asia. There they established colonies and other forms of political control that lasted, in some cases, until the middle of the 20th century.

Subordination to Western political control and cultural influences eventually contributed to a modern revival of Asian Buddhism beginning in the 1800s, during roughly the same time that Buddhism was introduced into the United States. Many Buddhists found new meaning in their ancient traditions as they responded to Western influences.

The notion of "strangeness" helps explain the history of Buddhism in the United States. The word "strange" comes from a Latin root meaning "foreign." As a religion, Buddhism is certainly foreign to the Western, biblical heritage of mainstream American culture. But "strange" also suggests something different, unusual, odd, or peculiar. Americans have viewed Buddhism at times with hostility and at others with fascination, both common responses to things that seem strange.

Two main groups in American history have followed this "strange" religion. One group consists of Asian Buddhist immigrants, who have been treated like "strangers" in a Europe-oriented America and have struggled to adapt their traditional religion to its new home in the United States. The second group consists of non-Asian Americans who have found Buddhism's "strangeness" intellectually stimulating and have chosen to explore this different path of spirituality.

America's "encounter with Buddhism," as one historian called it, started in the 1840s. Early in that decade, white Americans began to take notice of this ancient yet unfamiliar religion. Later in that same decade the first Buddhist immigrants arrived on American shores. The first encounter held a sense of fascination; the second brought forth a great deal of hostility.

In 1844 *The Dial,* a favorite magazine of a group of American intellectuals greatly interested in Eastern religions, published an English translation of a Buddhist sacred text. In the decades that followed, Buddhism continued to draw the attention of white Americans, although those who were interested did not always formally convert to the religion. The Theosophical Society, an organization with broad religious interests that was established in 1875, found Buddhism particularly attractive. As a result of a visit to Ceylon in 1880, both of the Society's founders vowed to follow Buddhism, and one of them, Colonel Henry

Olcott, is usually credited with designing the so-called Buddhist flag in use to this day.

Several books about Buddhism sold well among American readers. Among them were Edwin Arnold's *The Light of Asia* (1879), Olcott's *Buddhist Catechism* (1881), and Paul Carus's *The Gospel of Buddha* (1894). Although he was not a Buddhist, the U.S. scholar Henry Clarke Warren, author of *Buddhism in Translations* (1896), spoke of his fascination with Buddhism: "Now a large part of the pleasure that I have experienced in the study of Buddhism has arisen from the strangeness of what I call the intellectual landscape. All the ideas, the modes of argument, even the postulates assumed and not argued about, have always seemed so strange, so different from anything to which I have been accustomed, that I feel all the time as though walking in fairyland."

Copyright 1891

Colonel Henry Steel Olcott, American co-founder of the Theosophical Society, was greatly attracted to Buddhism.

Popular interest in Buddhism and other non-Western religions could be seen at the 1893 World's Parliament of Religions, held in Chicago as part of the Columbian Exposition, a fair that marked the 400th anniversary of Europe's discovery of the Americas. At times the event took on a carnival atmosphere, and several of the Asian representatives at the Parliament became objects of curiosity for Americans attending the Exposition. The newspaper accounts paid more attention to what the Asians wore than to the speeches they gave. One Buddhist priest in the Japanese delegation later reported that crowds sought them out wherever they went, shouting, "The Japanese are here! The Japanese are here!" and expressing a special fascination with their silk robes. The Parliament had to set up a separate "Buddhist Room" for the steady stream of visitors who wished to discuss the religion with particular Buddhist speakers. One of the most popular of these speakers was Kinzo Hirai, a Japanese layman who strongly criticized the United States for its treatment of Japanese immigrants. "[T]he claim is made that the Japanese are idolaters and heathen," Hirai observed. After listing many examples of U.S. mistreatment of Japanese immigrants, Hirai then proclaimed, "If such be the Christian ethics—well, we are perfectly satisfied to be heathen."

The Weaverville Joss House, an early Chinese Buddhist temple, in California in 1869. Chinese temples were often called joss houses because of the images of gods found in them; "joss" comes from the Portuguese word *deos* (god) used by early traders from Portugal in East Asia.

Public curiosity about Buddhism continued after the 1893 Parliament. In an article in the *Atlantic Monthly* a year later, a Methodist minister wrote, "[O]f the religions of the East, Buddhism is the best known and most popularly appreciated." Buddhist centers for interested whites opened in several cities. The Maha Bodhi Society opened branches in Chicago, New York, and San Francisco beginning in 1897, and the Dharma Sangha, or followers, of Buddha was established in San Francisco in 1900. Japanese teachers arrived to offer Zen training to Americans, beginning in 1905 with the return of Soyen Shaku, who had attended the 1893 Parliament. Zen, which emphasizes meditation as the key practice of Buddhism, would become the favored Buddhist school among U.S. converts.

But although some Americans were fascinated with the religion of Buddhism, many others received Buddhist immigrants with hostility. Of the Buddhist immigrants from Asia, Chinese were the first to arrive, followed by Japanese.

Perhaps 2.5 million people left China between 1840 and 1900, a socially and politically unstable period in China's history. Beginning in 1848, many of them went to work on the sugarcane plantations of Hawaii, which later became a U.S. territory before being granted statehood. Others sought their fortunes in California, which they called Gam Saan, "Gold Mountain," referring especially to the discovery of gold at Sutter's mill in the foothills of the Sierra Nevadas that year. One young man in Guangzhou, China, wrote to his brother regarding California's lure: "Oh! Very rich country! I hear good many Americans and Europeans go there. Oh! They find gold very quickly, so I hear. . . . I feel as if I should like to go there very much. I think I shall go to California next summer."

In February 1849, just 55 Chinese lived in California; only five years later, the number had soared to more than 40,000. Most of the early Chinese immigrants were men who came over without their wives and families, and most never expected to remain permanently in the United States. Many initially worked the rivers or mines for gold, often under very difficult living conditions. As the gold rush subsided, the Chinese moved into many occupations, including agriculture, private businesses, and railroad building. The Central Pacific Railroad, for example, employed between 12,000 and 14,000 Chinese workers during the completion of the transcontinental railway in the 1860s.

California at first seemed to welcome the Chinese. In a speech before the California legislature in January 1852, the governor called them "one of the most worthy classes" of the recent arrivals to the state. But in the next few months and years, that same legislature passed a series of discriminatory acts aimed primarily at the Chinese, including an 1855 law called "An Act to Discourage the Immigration to this State of Persons Who Cannot Become Citizens Thereof." (A 1790 law said that only white people could become naturalized citizens.) Many Californians rode a wave of anti-immigrant or nativist feeling summed up by the slogan "California for Americans." Local newspapers regularly reported violent acts against Chinese, including beatings, robberies, and even murders. By the 1880s, by which time the Chinese population had spread to several states, a series of anti-Chinese riots swept through many cities in the West. In the face of intense prejudice and discrimination, the Chinese increasingly retreated into the relative safety of "ethnic islands" in many U.S. cities, the Chinatowns that can still be found today. The gleam of Gold Mountain had tarnished greatly.

National anti-Chinese sentiment peaked in 1882 when the U.S. Congress passed the Chinese Exclusion Act, which was extended in 1892 and made permanent in 1902. For the first time in American history, a specific ethnic group was legally prohibited from entering the country. In the next few decades, U.S. immigration policies would become more limiting in general, but lawmakers viewed Asians as especially undesirable. They were "strangers from a different shore," as a Japanese-American historian puts it, considered racially and culturally incapable of blending into the dominant group in U.S. society, Euro-Americans, the descendants of immigrants from Europe.

In 1910, U.S. authorities set up an immigrant detention center on Angel Island in San Francisco Bay to examine Chinese and other Asians seeking to enter the United States. Angel Island became more notorious for harsh conditions than was Ellis Island in New York harbor, where most European immigrants entered the country. "When we arrived," explained one newcomer to Angel Island, "they locked us up like criminals in compartments like the cages in the zoo."

The Immigration Act of 1917 cut the immigration of Asian laborers, and laws passed in the 1920s established a national origins system for accepting immigrants. Under this system, only a set number of immigrants from a given country could enter the United States each year. The Immigration Act of 1924 effectively closed off immigration from Asia by denying immigration to "aliens ineligible to citizenship." Under this law, only 100 immigrants could enter the United States each year from each Asian country, although many thousands could come from Britain and other northern and western European nations. The provision that allowed only 100 people to come to the United States from China or Japan annually was not intended to permit Asians to immigrate—it was meant for whites who had been born in those countries. Asians in the United States saw clearly that the new immigration law was aimed at them. An old Chinese businessman's remark at the time reflected the hurt: "They call us 'Chink.' They think we no good! America cut us off. No more come now, too bad!"

But Chinese culture—including Buddhism—had already taken root in the United States. In 1853, only a few years after the first Chinese immigrants reached Gold Mountain, the first Chinese temple in America,

Kong Chow Temple, opened in San Francisco's Chinatown. During the great earthquake of 1906, firemen dynamited this structure, hoping to stop the fires that were raging through the city. Before the temple was destroyed, its caretaker had time to remove only one item: a statue of Kuan Ti, an important Chinese deity. That statue was restored to its place of prominence on the altar of the rebuilt temple in 1909.

About a hundred miles northeast of San Francisco, in the foothills of the Sierra Nevadas, sits the town of Oroville. Chinese prospectors by the thousands flocked to Oroville, and by the 1870s the town ranked second only to San Francisco in its number of Chinese residents. The first Chinese temple in Oroville, a wooden structure built in the 1850s, burned down and was replaced in the 1860s by a temple com-

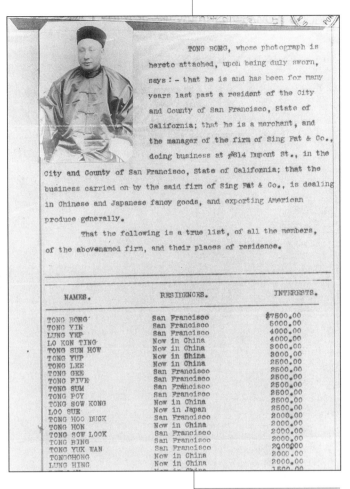

pound of brick buildings. These included the so-called Moon Temple, which took its name from a full-moon-shaped entryway and contained a beautiful golden statue of the Buddha, and the East Temple, with a private chapel for the wealthy Chinese family that had helped settle many of the early Chinese in Oroville. When Oroville prepared to celebrate the hundredth anniversary of its founding in 1948, the Oroville Women's Community Club, supported by both white and Chinese community leaders, led a project to renovate the temple buildings in time for the festivities. A Sacramento, California, newspaper quoted the opinion of an expert on Chinese culture concerning the quality of the work: "The Oroville Chinese Temple is without question the finest, most elaborate,

In 1902, the Immigration and Naturalization Service made this list of business partners in the Sing Fat Company, San Francisco, a Chinese trading firm. It was part of an investigation to certify the status of many Chinese immigrants as "merchants," a special category who, along with their wives and families, were exempt from Chinese exclusion laws.

Fifteen Buddhist priests carry staffs with Buddhist symbols in the funeral procession of Tom Kim Yung, a military attaché of the Chinese government, who committed suicide in 1903 following mistreatment by local police and bystanders in San Francisco.

and most extensive one in the entire state. Historically the temple is priceless." The temple had become a museum that recalled the contributions of Chinese settlers to the town's history, a cause for celebration for white and Chinese residents alike.

Religious practices in the Kong Chow and Oroville temples followed ancient Chinese popular or folk religion, which blends elements of Buddhism and native Chinese traditions. Next to statues of the Buddha stood ones of many Chinese deities. One was Kuan Ti, whose statue had been rescued from the Kong Chow Temple. Kuan Ti was known for his protective powers and as the god of prosperity, making him a favorite among Chinese immigrants who came seeking wealth in Gold Mountain but suffered persecution in the process. Chinese immigrants also practiced many rituals to honor their dead ancestors and to receive blessings from them.

Japanese immigrants began coming to the United States between 1868 and 1912, a time in Japanese history called the Meiji period. During this era of rapid modernization, Japan sought to "catch up" to the industrialized Western powers; at the same time, Japanese began emigrating to other lands. In 1870, 55 Japanese lived in the continental United States; by 1920 there were more than 100,000. Even more Japanese went to Hawaii. Most of the immigrants had been farmers in Japan, so many ended up working in agriculture in Hawaii and California. They intended to make their fortunes quickly and then return to Japan, but, as with the Chinese before them, most ended up staying permanently.

Anti-Japanese prejudice and discrimination mirrored the Chinese experience, particularly in California. "The racial antagonisms were so strong," writes Tetsuden Kashima, a sociologist whose father was a Japanese Buddhist priest in America, "that all spheres of Japanese life were attacked as alien or 'strange.'" One Japanese man related an experience during a visit to California in the 1920s. "In one instance, I went to a barber shop to get my hair trimmed," the man explained. "On entering the shop, one of the barbers approached me and asked for my nationality. I answered that I was Japanese, and as soon as he heard that I was of the yellow race, he drove me out of the place as if he were driving away a cat or a dog."

Many discriminatory legal actions were taken against Japanese immigrants in the early 1900s. In 1906 the San Francisco public school system attempted to segregate its Japanese and other Asian students from white students. The Japanese government lodged an official protest with President Theodore Roosevelt. The resulting negotiations produced the 1907–08 Gentlemen's Agreement between Japan and the United States, which included limits on the number of Japanese laborers who could come to the U.S. mainland. Between 1913 and the early 1920s, 11 states enacted so-called alien land laws to prevent noncitizens from owning land. These laws were aimed primarily at the Japanese, who could not become citizens because they were not white. The California law dramatically reduced the competition for land and profits faced by white farmers by forcing many neighboring Japanese farmers to move to urban areas, where they eventually established private business enterprises.

One celebrated court case involved a Japanese man's application for U.S. citizenship in 1914. Takao Ozawa had arrived in California in 1894. He graduated from a Berkeley high school, attended the University of California, and then worked for a U.S. company in Hawaii while raising a family. When Ozawa's citizenship application was turned down, he appealed this decision to a U.S. district court in 1916. The court denied the appeal, explaining that, although Ozawa was "in every way eminently qualified under the statutes to become an American citizen," he could not become one because he was not white. Ozawa appealed to the U.S. Supreme Court, arguing that he was "a true American" in every way. In 1922 the Supreme Court, in *Ozawa* v. *United*

States, also denied Ozawa's request based on his race.

Two years later, Congress passed an immigration act that barred persons ineligible for U.S. citizenship, which included several Asian nationalities. One Japanese immigrant reacted bitterly, noting the double standard he saw: "We try hard to be American but Americans always say you always Japanese. Irish become American and all time talk about Ireland; Italians become Americans even if do all time like in Italy; but Japanese can never be anything but Jap. I know I am not wanted. No use try to be American, we all have to go back to Japan some day."

Buddhist temples of the Jodo Shinshu school provided support for many Japanese immigrants during these trying times. An organization called the Young Men's Buddhist Association (YMBA) was established in San Francisco in 1899 through the joint efforts of two priests sent from Japan and 30 local Japanese residents. In 1914 the YMBA changed its name to the Buddhist Mission of North America (BMNA). By 1930 more than 30 temples, most of them in California, belonged to this denomination.

During their visit to the United States, the two priests who helped found the YMBA met in Seattle with the Japanese government's consul, who expressed concern about Buddhist missionary efforts in the United States. He feared that the United States would not welcome this "foreign religion." Some whites showed a positive interest in the religion during these years to the extent that the San Francisco temple even offered regular English-language services for them. Still, the predominant response to the Japanese—and their "strange" religion—was hostility. This seems to have led Reverend Koyu Uchida, director of the BMNA from 1905 to 1923, to encourage temples to adopt the name "church," a term familiar to U.S. Christians. Ironically, the hostility that Japanese immigrants endured seems to have fueled Buddhist missionary success among them, particularly after the passage of the 1924 Immigration Act. Some Japanese who had hesitated to identify themselves as Buddhists in a Christian land now began to assert their identities and rights.

Unlike the predominantly male Chinese immigrant community, many Japanese immigrants married and raised families in America. The period between 1908 and 1921 has been called the picture-bride era. In

Japan, thousands of women went through marriage ceremonies with stand-in grooms. They then crossed the Pacific Ocean to the United States to join their real husbands, who had chosen them on the basis of their photographs.

As the immigrant community grew, the wives of BMNA ministers often played a vital role in serving its spiritual and social needs. A tribute to Seto Uchida, wife of BMNA director Reverend Koyu Uchida, reads: "Mrs. Uchida, as many other [ministers'] wives, was a dedicated woman who toiled unselfishly with her husband for the Buddhist cause. She provided understanding and hospitality to the new ministers and other Buddhist followers upon their arrival in the United States."

Beginning around 1920 the BMNA began to address the special needs of the Nisei ("second") generation, the U.S.-born children of the immigrant or Issei ("first") generation. Historians of U.S. immigration have long recognized the so-called "problem" that the second generation of any immigrant group poses to its parents. Born and raised in U.S. society, the children quickly take on American cultural traits, and this American-

This racist woman was so strongly opposed to Asian immigration that she plastered her Los Angeles home with the message. In 1920s America, anti-Asian sentiment ran high.

ization may tempt them and their own children to forget the heritage that their immigrant parents treasured. As with other immigrant groups throughout U.S. history, the religious centers of Japanese communities began programs aimed at preserving ethnic pride and educating their children to be good Japanese Americans—not just good Japanese, not just good Americans, but both. The 1920s saw an upsurge in local Young Men's Buddhist Associations (YMBAs) and Young Women's Buddhist Associations (YWBAs), which offered cultural, educational, social, and athletic activities for the Nisei.

Of the more than 30 BMNA Buddhist churches in the continental United States by 1930, the Buddhist Church of San Francisco was the most historically significant. Not only was it the first Japanese Buddhist temple in the country, it also served as the BMNA's national headquarters. Because the original structure did not survive the great earthquake of 1906, a second was opened in 1914 and expanded in the late 1930s. The king of Siam (modern Thailand) presented the temple with some relics of great religious value, including ashes from the Buddha's cremation ceremony, which were enshrined in a sacred, domed enclosure on the roof of the building. At the time, this was the only Buddhist reliquary shrine outside Asia.

Most of the early BMNA temples did not stand out markedly from their surroundings, many being former Christian churches that the immigrant community had bought. They were, however, decorated with Buddhist symbols. Perhaps the most common one was the Wheel of the Dharma ("Teaching"), its eight spokes representing the Noble Eightfold Path to Nirvana as taught by the Buddha. The lotus plant was another common symbol. Its ability to rise above muddy water symbolizes an enlightened mind uncontaminated by the evils of the world. One symbol more common before World War II than after it was the swastika. In Buddhism and other ancient Asian religions, the swastika has a meaning quite unrelated to the ideology of Nazi Germany, which adopted the symbol as its own. For Buddhists the swastika represents a worldly existence that they seek to transcend through spiritual practices and upright moral behavior.

Strangers from a Different Shore

In his books, the third-generation Japanese-American historian Ronald Takaki describes how Asian Americans have felt like strangers in the United States because of their racial identities and cultural heritages. Here Takaki speaks of one such experience of his own.

I had flown from San Francisco to Norfolk and was riding in a taxi to my hotel to attend a conference on multiculturalism. Hundreds of educators from across the country were meeting to discuss the need for greater cultural diversity in the curriculum. My driver and I chatted about the weather and the tourists. The sky was cloudy, and Virginia Beach was twenty minutes away. The rearview mirror reflected a white man in his forties. "How long have you been in this country?" he asked. "All my life," I replied, wincing. "I was born in the United States." With a strong southern drawl, he remarked: "I was wondering because your English is excellent!" Then, as I had many times before, I explained: "My grandfather came here from Japan in the 1880s. My family has been here, in America, for over a hundred years." He glanced at me in the mirror. Somehow I did not look "American" to him; my eyes and complexion looked foreign. . . .

Asian Americans have been here for over 150 years, before many European immigrant groups. But as "strangers" coming from a "different shore," they have been stereotyped as "heathen," exotic, and unassimilable. Seeking "Gold Mountain," the Chinese arrived first, and what happened to them influenced the reception of the Japanese, Koreans, Filipinos, and Asian Indians as well as the Southeast Asian refugees like the Vietnamese and the Hmong.

In the Buddhist Room of the Museum of Fine Arts, early-20th-century Bostonians could learn about the religion. During the early 1900s, Boston's intellectuals made their city a center of American interest in Buddhism and East Asian culture.

Inside the BMNA temples, the focal point was an altar or series of altars holding many Buddhist symbols and images. The most important of these was a statue of Amida Buddha, who is not the same as the historical Buddha but a spiritual being to whom worshipers look for help in reaching an ultimate state of bliss and enlightenment called the Pure Land. For instance, members of the San Luis Obispo Buddhist Church, established in 1927, would assemble before the altar during the fall festival of Higan-E to contemplate the balance found in the natural world and to seek a similar balance in their own lives. "Therefore we gather before the sacred shrine of Amida Buddha," they would recite, "and meditate on the harmony of nature and devote ourselves to the realization of this harmony in our inner lives."

Death marks a traumatic passage in human life, and Buddhism offers rituals that lend meaning to the death experience for both the dying person and his or her loved ones. Such rituals were especially comforting when Japanese immigrants died away from their homeland. Funeral services, whether in the home or at the Buddhist temple, carried both spiritual and cultural significance and stressed the hope for rebirth in the blissful Pure Land of Amida Buddha. Typically, the body was cremated and the ashes placed in a commemorative area of the temple. Memorial services for the deceased would take place on certain dates, such as the hundredth day and the first year after the death.

America's encounter with Buddhism began with a mixture of fascination and hostility. The dual response to the "strangeness" of this Asian religion would continue to characterize the history of Buddhism in the United States. Between the restrictive immigration laws of the 1920s and the reversal of such trends beginning in the 1940s, ethnic-Asian Buddhists would continue to adapt to life in the United States, while some non-Asian Americans would maintain their interest in Buddhism.

Chapter 2

Buddhists Adapt and Explore

The laws excluding immigrants of various countries that were passed in the early part of the 20th century brought Asian emigration to the United States to a near standstill from the late 1920s to the mid-1940s. During these years the immigrant Buddhist communities already in the United States—mostly Chinese and Japanese—settled into the task of adapting to their new home. "For some time," explained Reverend Koyu Uchida, director of the Buddhist Mission of North America in the early 1900s, "special emphasis has been laid on the necessity of the Americanization of our people, and all the clergy located at different churches [temples] strive to educate the members in the American way of life." But the Americanization of the Japanese in these years took on a unique poignancy. Despite their efforts to blend into American society, Japanese living in the United States would face the harsh reality of their "differentness" when the United States entered into a war with Japan in 1941.

The growth of the Nisei (second) generation of immigrants from Japan after 1920 accounts for much of the adaptation seen at Japanese Buddhist temples during this period. Buddhists borrowed Christian terminology and approaches, while some traditional Buddhist practices underwent a process that became known as Protestantization, in which they came to resemble America's dominant religion, Protestant Christianity. For instance, many temples began to offer programs of Buddhist Sunday schools patterned after their Christian counterparts, while the Young

Prisoners at the Granada Relocation Center in Amache, Colorado, dance at a Bon Odori festival dance that the Granada Buddhist Church sponsored. The party was held at night on the center's baseball diamond.

Men's Buddhist Associations and Young Women's Buddhist Associations organized by Issei or first-generation parents in the 1920s continued to offer activities for Nisei youth similar to the Christian models, the YMCA and YWCA. In 1937 Nisei leaders, who now outnumbered their Issei elders in the YMBAs and YWBAs, formed the Young Buddhist Association (YBA) for both male and female members, rejecting their parents' more conservative views about separating the sexes for social activities.

Buddhist religious services began to resemble Protestant Christian worship in some ways. Unlike most ministers in Japan, Buddhist ministers in America related to their congregations in a somewhat democratic fashion, like other American clergy. The hymnbooks and ritual handbooks used in U.S. temples took on a Protestant tone. Reverend Ernest Hunt, an Anglican Christian in Hawaii who converted to Buddhism, compiled a popular book of ceremonies in English. It included *gathas* or Buddhist songs written by his wife, Dorothy, that sounded very much like Protestant hymns. Another influential convert, Reverend Julius Goldwater—who was formerly Jewish—wrote a ritual handbook that included Dorothy Hunt's hymns, with catechisms (texts to teach Buddhist doctrines to children) and services for weekly religious gatherings and special occasions such as marriages and funerals. One hymn, entitled "Buddha's Soldiers," sung to the tune of "Battle Hymn of the Republic," substituted Buddhist sentiments for the Christian lyrics—for instance, a refrain worded as "The Dharma's marching on" instead of the original "His [God's] truth is marching on." One reading for the celebration of the Buddha's birth clearly reflected the style of the Sermon on the Mount in the Christian New Testament, with lines like "Blessed are they that reject evil / For they shall attain purity" and "Blessed are they that follow the path / For they shall attain enlightenment."

A survey conducted in the San Francisco area in 1934 found that Japanese Buddhist parents tended to give American rather than Japanese names to their children and were raising them without the Buddhist ceremonies of childhood traditionally performed in Japan. Religious weddings, not a part of traditional Japanese Buddhism, became popular among Japanese Americans and took on the style of Christian ceremonies. Buddhist religious holidays, such as those commemorating key events in the life of the Buddha, were still celebrated in traditional ways, along with U.S. observances like the Fourth of July, Halloween, Thanksgiving, and even the Christian holy day of Christmas.

In 1930 several prominent Nisei businessmen and professionals established the Japanese American Citizens League (JACL) to give national expression to the Americanization of the Nisei generation. James Sakamoto, editor of a Japanese-American newspaper, wrote, "The time is here to give a little sober thought to the future. The second generation are American citizens and through them will be reaped the harvests of tomorrow. Home, institutions, and inalienable rights to live the life of an American, is the cry of the second generation and will be the cry of posterity."

The JACL grew quickly, claiming 5,600 members and 50 affiliate chapters nationwide by 1940. The organization stressed economic self-improvement and pride in America. Sakamoto wrote that "only if the second generation as a whole works to inculcate in all its members the true spirit of American patriotism can the group escape the unhappy fate of being a clan apart from the rest of American life." Of course, not all Nisei

A U.S. Army soldier stands with his mother in their family's strawberry field in Sacramento County, California. The son had been furloughed to help his family prepare for relocation during World War II. The government relocated more than 450 Japanese-American families from this vicinity in 1942.

wished to give up their Japanese identity completely and become exclusively "American."

Moreover, most recognized that their racial difference from the majority of Americans was a barrier to full acceptance, even though all Nisei were American citizens, because they had been born in the United States. Japan's bombing of the U.S. naval base at Pearl Harbor, Hawaii, in December 1941 dramatically highlighted Japanese Americans' barrier to full acceptance. That act of military aggression drew the United States into World War II. It also created an atmosphere of wartime distrust in the United States that, combined with years of anti-Japanese sentiment, turned American public opinion against Japanese people within the country. Many viewed Japanese Americans as potential internal threats to national security. On February 19, 1942, President Franklin D. Roosevelt signed Executive Order 9066, which gave the U.S. Army authority to relocate Japanese and Japanese Americans on the West Coast. The War Relocation Authority incarcerated them in so-called relocation centers in seven states. A total of 120,000 people were relocated, two-thirds of them U.S. citizens and three-fourths of them under the age of 25. The camps operated between 1942 and 1946.

Norman Mineta was born in San Jose, California, in 1931 and was incarcerated in 1942. Reflecting on the 50th anniversary of the bombing of Pearl Harbor, Mineta wrote in 1991:

> I remember being struck for the first time by the stigma of disloyalty written into the notices that the Army had posted throughout the West Coast. The signs addressed us as "aliens and non-aliens." Imagine. Even though I was born a citizen in the United States, the only status my government would grant me was the rank of "non-alien."

In 1971 Mineta became the first Japanese-American mayor of a major U.S. city, San Jose, California; in 1974 he was the first Japanese-American congressman elected from a mainland state; and in 2000 President George W. Bush made him Secretary of Transportation.

In her memoir, *Farewell to Manzanar,* Jeanne Wakatsuki Houston shared her experiences as a young girl in the relocation center in Manzanar, California:

We had pulled up just in time for dinner. The mess halls weren't completed yet. An outdoor chow line snaked around a half-finished building that broke a good part of the wind. They issued us army mess kits, the round metal kind that fold over, and plopped in scoops of canned Vienna sausage, canned string beans, steamed rice that had been cooked too long, and on top of the rice a serving of canned apricots. The Caucasian servers were thinking that the fruit poured over rice would make a good dessert. Among the Japanese, of course, rice is never eaten with sweet foods, only with salty or savory foods. Few of us could eat such a mixture. But at this point no one dared protest. It would have been impolite.

Government actions often underscored the plight of the incarcerated population. For instance, in early 1943 the War Relocation Authority included a loyalty test in its application for clearance to leave the camps. Two questions—about abiding by the laws of the United States and being willing to serve in the U.S. armed forces on behalf of the war effort—caused confusion in the minds of many prisoners. For the Issei, did loyalty to the United States mean denying their Japanese homeland and heritage? And what type of loyalty could be expected when the United States had already denied them the basic right of citizenship? The Nisei wondered what type of loyalty was to be expected when the United States had suspended their constitutional rights as citizens. Even so, the great majority of prisoners answered yes to the questions. For them, the process of being released from the camps began later that year. Many eventually settled in large cities in the eastern United States. Also in 1943, a force of Nisei soldiers was formed. The 442nd Regimental Combat Team distinguished itself as one of the most decorated fighting units in American history.

The incarceration experience profoundly affected the entire Japanese-American community. About 31 percent of the internees were Christians; more than 55 percent were Buddhists. Families were forced to leave their homes and businesses on short notice, storing their belongings at local Buddhist temples and in Christian churches. Reverend Julius Goldwater acted as caretaker of three such temples in the Los Angeles area during the relocation years.

The relocation centers brought Buddhists of various traditions together, although most came from Buddhist Mission of North America

These Buddhist baby boomers, children born soon after the end of World War II, parade in traditional Japanese robes in New York City in 1953.

(BMNA) temples. Tensions arose at times among the different Buddhist groups, and compromises were often necessary to accommodate the variety of practices and beliefs among the prisoners. Some Buddhist leaders sought closer unity by forming inter-Buddhist organizations like the United Buddhist Church and the Buddhist Brotherhood of America. The BMNA emerged from the relocation experience as a new organization, the Buddhist Churches of America (BCA), established in 1944.

The BCA brought a major shift toward Americanization. Formal ties with Japan diminished, the use of English in temple activities increased, and the younger generation of Nisei took over the official leadership of the national organization. Decades later, as the BCA celebrated the 100th anniversary of its founding as the Young Men's Buddhist Association, some within the denomination questioned whether Americanization had gone too far, and discussions arose as to whether the BCA should substitute a Buddhist term for the Christian-derived word "Churches" in its official name. However, no official name change occurred.

After incarceration, most Japanese returned to their communities on the West Coast, but others settled elsewhere and established new Buddhist temples. In 1944, two temples opened in Chicago: Midwest Buddhist Temple and Buddhist Temple of Chicago. In the early 1970s, Midwest, a BCA affiliate, built its present facility in the upscale Lincoln Park neighborhood. It is Chicago's only newly constructed immigrant Buddhist temple. Buddhist Temple of Chicago's founder, Reverend Gyomay Kubose, a leader in inter-Buddhist cooperation during his incarceration at the Heart Mountain, Wyoming, relocation center, believed that the various traditional schools of Asian Buddhism should complement each other in creating a new American version of Buddhism.

World War II was a turning point in the history of U.S. ethnic relations. Many Americans were aware of the contradiction in fighting a war against a racist Nazi regime in Germany while racist attitudes and policies still prevailed in the United States. As 1940 Republican Presidential candidate Wendell Willkie put it, "Today it is becoming increasingly apparent to thoughtful Americans that we cannot fight the forces of imperialism abroad and maintain a form of imperialism at home." The civil rights movement that flowered in the African-American community during the 1950s and 1960s had origins in 1940s protests against racial discrimination, especially labor union leader A. Philip Randolph's threats of massive marches on Washington over employment practices in defense factories and segregation in the U.S. armed forces.

This new social atmosphere brought an easing of restrictions on

This page from a scrapbook records a child's days at a Buddhist summer camp in upstate New York in the 1950s. Summer camp gave children a chance to learn the arts of their ethnic heritage, such as traditional Japanese pen and ink sketching, and strengthened their sense of a Buddhist community.

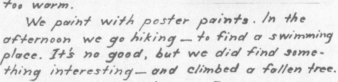

tricks — and did ourselves.

Rev. Yoshikami had really surprised his family in coming. Now the men have all returned to the City, even Mr. Sumi. Our lady guests too — and Mrs. Karasawa with Jaunita, but they are coming back. We need their car.

Monday, August 11 — It's sunny — and a little too warm.

We paint with poster paints. In the afternoon we go hiking — to find a swimming place. It's no good, but we did find something interesting — and climbed a fallen tree.

Tuesday, August 12 — For class, we made little dolls from woolen yarn. Sure sounds sissy, but it was fun.

Paul's mother, Mrs. Okuno — came today. The older girls were waiting so that she could teach them pen and ink sketching.

Asian immigration and a more positive view of Asians in America. In 1943 Congress repealed the Chinese Exclusion Act of 1882 and gave Chinese immigrants the right to become naturalized U.S. citizens. Public opinion of Chinese people had improved largely because China fought with the United States on the Allied side in the war against Japan. Also influential in reshaping American attitudes was a successful 1943 tour of the United States by Madame Chiang Kai-Shek, wife of the political and military leader of Nationalist China, Generalissimo Chiang Kai-shek. In 1952 Congress passed the McCarran-Walter Act, which granted citizenship rights to Japanese immigrants. One historian has described the changes in immigration law and policy after World War II as a "door" to the United States. All but closed to Asians by the exclusionary legislation of the late 1800s and early 1900s, the door opened a little between the 1940s and 1965.

Even so, anti-Asian sentiment lingered. Speaking in support of a 1946 bill to allow a few immigrants each year from India and the Philippines, both of which had been U.S. allies in the war, Representative Clare Boothe Luce of Connecticut qualified her stance by saying, "I hope I make it clear that I would be the first to protest against people from any nation, of any color, coming here in such numbers as to lower our living standards and weaken our culture." She went on to point out that having too many Asians—"Orientals" in her words—posed a particular threat, because their ways differed substantially from those of the majority culture in the United States: "We are utterly justified in controlling and keeping low Oriental immigration in terms of numbers, because of the fact that they in too great numbers may undermine our way of life, our living standards, our form of religion."

While ethnic-Asian Buddhists practiced and adapted their traditional religion, non-Asian Americans continued to explore Buddhism between the 1930s and the 1960s. Whites such as Ernest and Dorothy Hunt and Julius Goldwater had been studying Buddhism with the Japanese Jodo Shinshu community in Hawaii since the 1920s. Beginning in the late 1940s, Reverend Gyomay Kubose's Buddhist Temple of Chicago drew as many as 30 whites to weekly services.

Zen Buddhism attracted the most converts, largely through the efforts of Japanese teachers who set up meditation centers in major U.S. cities. Two followers of Soyen Shaku, a delegate to the 1893 World's Parliament of Religions, opened important centers in the 1930s. One of these followers was Shigetsu Sasaki, also known as Sokei-an, who founded the Buddhist Society of America in New York City in 1931. Sokei-an once remarked that establishing Zen Buddhism in America would be as difficult as getting a lotus plant to take root on a rock—it would require many patient years of holding the lotus to the rock. After his death in 1945, Sokei-an's American wife, Ruth Fuller Sasaki, carried on his work at the New York center, now called the First Zen Institute of America.

The other notable follower of Soyen Shaku to come to the United States and open an important center was Nyogen Senzaki, who opened

The Young Buddhist Association (YBA) baseball team of the New York Buddhist Church, a Buddhist Churches of America (BCA) temple, in 1950. YBAs organized social activities for the American-born generations of Japanese-American Buddhists.

his Zen center in San Francisco, then moved it to Los Angeles in 1931. Senzaki taught two separate congregations interested in Zen, one Japanese, one white. During World War II, Senzaki was incarcerated at Heart Mountain, Wyoming, where he held meditation sessions in his small cabin with a few prisoners. Senzaki often called America "this strange land." One of Senzaki's U.S. students, Robert Aitken, played an important role in the spread of Zen during the 1960s, which some have called the Zen Decade. Noticing that many young, counterculture meditators were taking psychedelic substances like LSD and mescaline, Aitken opened a Zen center in Maui, Hawaii, where they could explore new states of consciousness without drugs.

If the 1960s was the Zen Decade for American converts, the 1950s had paved the way with its own "Zen Boom." The Japanese scholar D. T. Suzuki gave an influential series of lectures on Zen at Columbia University in New York, and in 1957 he participated in a conference on Zen Buddhism and psychoanalysis with such leading psychologists as Erich Fromm. A *New Yorker* magazine profile of Suzuki in 1957 pointed to Zen's current popularity in the West, suggesting that it had become a "movement of considerable importance."

Around this time a literary circle called the Beat Generation adopted aspects of Zen Buddhism into their lifestyle, with poets Allen Ginsberg and Gary Snyder and novelist Jack Kerouac leading the way. At one point Kerouac predicted that the President of the United States would someday meditate in a meditation room in the White House. The 1990s brought a revival of interest in Beat Generation literature, and Kerouac's Buddhist manuscripts were published. One was "Wake Up," a biography of the Buddha written in 1955. "I have designed this to be a handbook for Western understanding of the ancient [Buddhist] Law," Kerouac wrote in his author's note at the beginning of the manuscript. "The purpose is to convert. May I live up to these words. . . . " Kerouac's published works on Buddhism were not always appreciated during his lifetime, however. One reviewer called his 1958 book *The Dharma Bums* "the Gospel according to St. Kerouac," criticizing its simplistic presentation of Zen.

By the mid-1960s, Zen practitioners could be found throughout the

Buddha: More Than a Statue

Novelist Jack Kerouac was one of the Beat generation writers attracted to Buddhism in the 1950s. The description that follows is from his imaginative biography of the Buddha, entitled Wake Up, *written in 1955 but unpublished until the Beat generation revival of the 1990s.*

Buddha means the awakened one.

Until recently most people thought of the Buddha as a big fat rococo sitting figure with his belly out, laughing, as represented in millions of tourist trinkets and dime-store statuettes here in the Western world. People didn't know that the actual Buddha was a handsome young prince who suddenly began brooding in his father's palace, staring through the dancing girls as though they weren't there, at the age of twenty-nine, till finally and emphatically he threw up his hands and rode out to the forest on his war horse and cut off his long golden hair with his sword and sat down with the holy men of the India of his day and died at the age of eighty a lean venerable wanderer of ancient roads and elephant woods. This man was no slob-like figure of mirth, but a serious and tragic prophet, the Jesus Christ of India and almost all Asia.

Allen Ginsberg, Timothy Leary, and Ralph Metzner (left to right) in front of a large Buddha statue prior to a "psychedelic celebration" at New York City's Village Theater in the 1960s. Ginsberg was a key transitional figure between the Beat Generation of the 1950s and the counterculture of the 1960s.

United States. Major centers opened in New York City, Rochester, N.Y., Boston, Philadelphia, Washington, D.C., Chicago, Los Angeles, San Francisco, and Hawaii. The founder of the Zen Center of Los Angeles, Taizan Maezumi-Roshi, trained a generation of U.S. Zen masters, who incorporate their teacher's concern for active spirituality in their own centers today. John Daido Loori, for instance, founded the Zen Mountain Monastery, in New York's Catskill Mountains, which runs a meditation program for prisoners and a center for environmental studies. Bernard Tetsugen Glassman started a bakery and an apartment building to help poor residents in New York City. Glassman writes that "going to the Zendo [meditation hall] or the temple or the church is a beautiful thing, but we should be careful not to fall into the trap of thinking that the temple is the only place you can practice your religion."

Another influential Zen teacher, Shunryu Suzuki, came to San Francisco in 1959 to serve as the priest of a Japanese temple called the Soto Zen Mission. Non-Japanese Americans soon took to his style of meditation practice, which emphasized proper posture in seated meditation while seeking the Buddhist goal of enlightenment. By the late 1960s Suzuki's work resulted in the establishment of the inner-city San Francisco Zen Center and a remarkable retreat facility called Zen Mountain Center at Tassajara Hot Springs in California's Los Padres National Forest. Both the spirituality and the food offered at the Zen Mountain Center appealed to young people in the 1960s who had turned to eastern religions and wished to live a more "natural" lifestyle.

Most of the non-Asian Americans who have been attracted to Buddhism have been white. One exception is the multiethnic success of a Buddhist group that follows the teachings of a 13th-century Japanese figure named Nichiren Daishonin. The headquarters of Nichiren Shoshu of America opened in Los Angeles in 1963. This group's followers chant a simple ritual phrase, *Nam-myoho-renge-kyo.* They believe it has life-changing power, as portrayed, for instance, in the film biography of the pop singer Tina Turner, "What's Love Got To Do With It?" Recently this movement split into two groups, one called Soka Gakkai International, the other keeping the original Nichiren Shoshu name. Combined they may claim more U.S.-convert members today than any other single Buddhist school.

By the mid-1960s, the third phase of Buddhism in the United States was about to dawn. Between 1965 and the end of the 20th century, American interest in the religion would continue to grow, and Asian immigration would reach an all-time high, bringing new waves of Buddhists to America's shores.

Chapter 3

Buddhism's Growth and Popularity

Today, more Americans either practice Buddhism or express positive views about it than at any other time in U.S. history. This is largely the result of two important social trends that began in the 1960s: the ending of immigration restrictions against Asians, and the religious dissatisfactions of many Americans born after World War II.

The "baby-boomers," as they came to be called, grew into a generation of spiritual seekers. Some who had been raised as Christians or Jews sought alternative identities among the many new religious movements that sprouted in the 1960s and later, including several Buddhist groups new to the United States. A 1998 book called *The Complete Guide to Buddhist America* highlighted the dramatic increase in the practice of Buddhist meditation, listing nearly 1,100 meditation centers throughout the United States and Canada, 98 percent of them founded since 1965 and 58 percent since 1985.

Sandy Boucher, author of *Turning the Wheel*, a book about American Buddhist women, may speak for many men and women in telling her story of moving from a Methodist upbringing to a Buddhist worldview. Boucher recalls feeling that during her first experience meditating, at the Tassajara Zen retreat center in California in the early 1980s, "I wanted never to leave that place, for I experienced a profound peacefulness."

Worshipers at a southern California temple take turns bathing the baby Buddha during a celebration of his birthday.

In the 1990s, Buddhism became a common topic for conversation in chic circles, recalling its similar popularity in the 1890s and during the Zen boom of the 1950s. Media attention abounded. *USA Today, Time, Newsweek, People,* and the *Christian Science Monitor* all ran articles on Buddhism's revival. Oprah Winfrey devoted one episode of her television show to the story of a Seattle boy thought to be the reincarnation, or rebirth, of a great Tibetan Buddhist teacher. Such treatments typically included lists of high-profile "celebrity Buddhists" such as the Dalai Lama, the exiled leader of one school of Tibetan Buddhism, and entertainers Richard Gere, Steven Seagal, Tina Turner, and the Beastie Boys' Adam Yauch. "Buddhism is everywhere," declared a 1997 *New York Times* report titled "Buddhism's Flowering in America." That same year *Self* magazine asked, "What exactly is Buddhism, and why is it so hip now?" Comedian Robin Williams complimented 1998 Academy Award–winner Jack Nicholson as being "more cool than Buddha," and basketball superstar Michael Jordan explained that in a Chicago Bulls win over the Utah Jazz in the 1998 NBA finals he "just decided to use a little Zen Buddhism and relax instead of being frustrated, just smile and let it flow." Jordan had learned about Zen from his coach, Phil Jackson, whose book *Sacred Hoops* presents Jackson's philosophy of spiritually motivated basketball.

Zen Buddhism continued to attract the most interest among American seekers, though schools from the Vajrayana branch of Buddhism gained popularity beginning in the 1970s. For instance, Shambhala International, founded originally as Vajradhatu in 1973 by Tibetan teacher Chogyam Trungpa Rinpoche, now operates more than 100 meditation centers worldwide as well as an accredited liberal arts college called the Naropa Institute, in Boulder, Colorado. Interest in *vipassana,* the practice of insight meditation in the Theravada branch of Buddhism, has also increased since the 1970s. One important group, the Insight Meditation Society, established in 1975 in Barre, Massachusetts, has influenced the teaching and meditation styles of many *vipassana* centers around the country. Independent Buddhist groups have appeared in recent years as well. *Tricycle: The Buddhist Review,* a magazine for Americans interested in Buddhism, began publication in 1991. *Tricycle* sponsors an annual Change

Your Mind Day in New York City's Central Park, featuring meditation practices from various Buddhist schools. As the magazine's editor told the *New York Times,* "The miracle, if you get into it, is you can have a couple of thousand people in New York City and it can get very, very quiet."

The American-convert side of Buddhism faced a difficult time of transition in the 1980s when several important teachers died and improper sexual activities and abuse of authority by some key leaders

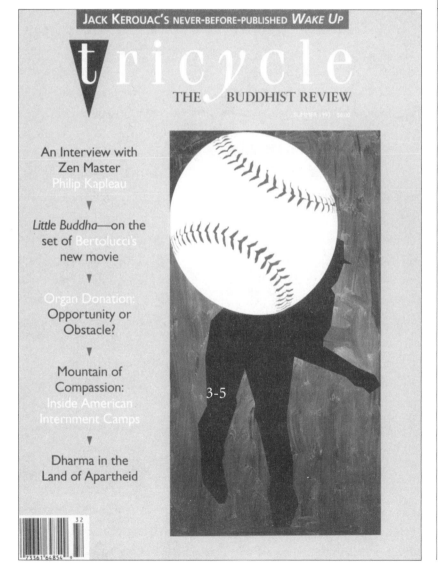

JACK KEROUAC'S NEVER-BEFORE-PUBLISHED *WAKE UP*

tricycle

THE BUDDHIST REVIEW

An Interview with
Zen Master
Philip Kapleau

▼

Little Buddha—on the
set of Bertolucci's
new movie

▼

Organ Donation:
Opportunity or
Obstacle?

▼

Mountain of
Compassion:
Inside American
Internment Camps

▼

Dharma in the
Land of Apartheid

3-5

Tricycle: The Buddhist Review appeals to an American audience of Buddhist converts and others interested in Buddhist beliefs and practices. In its summer 1993 issue, *Tricycle's* editor noted several intriguing numerical coincidences between Buddhism and baseball, the American pastime, including an equal number of stitches on a baseball and beads on a Buddhist prayer rosary—108.

came to light. As one Buddhist observer put it, the 1980s marked both a "changing of the guard" in leadership and a "period of adolescence" from which American-convert Buddhism as a whole would emerge in more mature form. But some non-Buddhist observers took a stance against a revitalized Buddhist presence in the 1990s. An editor of the evangelical magazine *Christianity Today* warned Christians in 1990 about "dabbling in the danger zone" of eastern religions like Buddhism; four years later the magazine ran a story about the disturbing trend it saw, entitled "America becoming fertile mission field for Buddhism." In fact, the number of actual converts to Buddhism by the 1990s remained small in comparison to the total number of U.S. Christians. In a poll reported in the *Los Angeles Times* in 1996, out of 1,000 randomly telephoned adults, 33 percent labeled Buddhism a negative influence on U.S. society. Only atheism and Scientology were ranked higher. Four percent of respondents considered Christianity to be a negative influence.

The second influence on contemporary American Buddhism has been the arrival of new Asian immigrants. In 1965 Congress passed the Hart-Celler Act, expanding the openings created between 1943 and 1952 for Buddhists and others from Asian countries to enter the United States. More than a third of all legal immigrants during the 1970s and 1980s came from Asia. New Asian Buddhist populations joined the Chinese and Japanese Buddhists already living in the United States. Many new immigrant Buddhist temples opened, including the Buddhist Vihara in Washington, D.C., the first Sri Lankan temple in the country (1966); Wat Thai of Los Angeles, the first Thai temple (1972); Wat Lao Phouthavong in Catlett, Virginia, the first Laotian temple (1979); and Wat Buddhikarama in Silver Spring, Maryland, the first Cambodian temple (1979). Hundreds of temples representing several ethnic-Asian groups now dot the urban landscape of America because of this influx of new immigrants.

The diversity of backgrounds within ethnic-Asian Buddhism today is remarkable. The first immigrant wave after the 1965 act included many professionals and highly educated people. Later waves brought some less-skilled and less-educated immigrants, as well as many refugees from war-torn Buddhist countries in Southeast Asia. These factors explain why

some Buddhist groups struggle to survive in America today while others have adjusted quite successfully to their new homeland.

The overall Chinese-American population of the United States more than quadrupled between 1965 and 1990. As a whole, recent Chinese immigrants, especially those from Taiwan, have tended to enjoy economic success. Perhaps the most magnificent Buddhist temple in the western hemisphere was built in suburban Los Angeles by a group headquartered in Taiwan. The temple's name, Hsi Lai, means "coming to the West." Its opening in Hacienda Heights in 1988 drew press notices in *Life* and the *New York Times Magazine*. Built at a cost of more than $30 million, the Hsi Lai Temple complex houses dozens of Buddhist monks and nuns and serves tens of thousands of local Chinese and other Buddhists. A 1996 visit to the temple by Vice President Al Gore stirred controversy over the Democratic National Committee's fundraising practices. *Time* magazine's

Buddhists participate in a walking meditation session in the courtyard of Hsi Lai Temple in suburban Los Angeles. Whether in a walking or sitting mode, Buddhists meditate to gain clarity and peace of mind.

photo of Chinese nuns testifying before a U.S. Senate committee brought unwanted notoriety to immigrant Buddhism in general and the Hsi Lai Temple in particular.

At the other end of the social spectrum are newcomers from some Southeast Asian Buddhist countries who have struggled since coming to America. Hundreds of thousands of refugees fled Vietnam, Laos, and Cambodia following the end of the Vietnam War in 1975. Many eventually settled in the United States. The typical refugee experience differs greatly from that of voluntary immigrants: refugees have been forced out of their homelands under difficult circumstances and must enter strange new countries with few resources and often minimal education and skills.

Cambodian Americans illustrate the difficulties of the refugee experience. In 1970, when the war in Vietnam spilled over into neighboring Cambodia, almost no Cambodians lived in the United States. About a decade later, however, the U.S. government began resettling thousands of

Women light candles and incense at the Buddha altar in Wat Buddhikakhemararama, a Cambodian temple in Long Beach, California. At the end of the 20th century, southern California had the largest concentration of Cambodian Americans in the United States.

Cambodian refugees here, and by 1990 the U.S. census reported nearly 150,000 Cambodians in the country (probably fewer than the actual total). Medical workers in the Cambodian-American community report many cases of post-traumatic stress disorder (mental and physical problems resulting from severe distress, as in war or torture) and other health problems linked to the tragedies the refugees endured. One survey estimated that 84 percent of Cambodian households in California had at least one person under medical supervision. Four of every 10 Cambodian families in the United States live below the poverty income level, and half receive some form of public financial aid. Their unemployment rates are high, and Cambodians often qualify only for low-paying, low-prestige jobs. Social problems, particularly strains between immigrant parents and their American-raised children, weaken the community.

The 1991 film *Rebuilding the Temple* portrays the difficulties of Cambodian-American life. In this movie a Cambodian describes the refugee experience: "I look out on this great country and am overwhelmed with grief. It makes me pity my own country, shattered and burning with war. Americans live with their loved ones, we are scattered around the world. Because of the madness of a few, we must seek shelter far from home. We no longer know happiness, only sadness. Will we ever see our homeland again? Or will we stay in this country forever, singing the refugee song?"

As the camera shows young Cambodian Americans hanging out in a public park, one man comments: "In Cambodia . . . the family members were very close together, dependent on each other. Over here you have an open society, you have so much freedom here that Cambodian parents are having a hard time in showing the traditional way. . . . So the children are torn between the two worlds, and that is the problem."

Like other Buddhist groups before them—and like American groups of all religious identities—Cambodian Americans hope to maintain their traditional values and customs by establishing religious centers. Only a handful of Cambodian Buddhist temples existed in the United States before 1980, but now there are more than 50. As one man living in Massachusetts put it, "We want to build temples so that the Cambodians in

Why We Attend the Buddhist Vihara

For the 25th anniversary of the founding of the Washington, D.C., Buddhist Vihara, the first Sri Lankan Buddhist temple in the United States, Senarath, a member of that congregation, reflected on why his family attends the temple.

Recently on a Sunday afternoon we were getting ready to go to the Washington Vihara when we had a visitor, a friend of our family. He asked us why we had to go to the Vihara and argued that one does not need to attend the Vihara to be a good Buddhist. He implied that it was mostly habit or guilt.

After he left we thought about some of the reasons that are given for not attending the Vihara. The most common of them are: Sundays are the only days I have to be with my family; the *pirith* [or *pirit,* sacred verses] and sermons are too long and boring; Sunday service conflicts with my favorite sport or TV program; the priests are not so good; I am too busy; I do not have time; etc. etc.

It did not take us too long to come up with many good reasons for going to the Vihara.

Observing the five precepts and meditating for a few minutes—with the inner peace this experience gives us—are the foremost reasons for attending the Vihara.

Participating in religious services helps us grow spiritually. The Vihara provides a pious atmosphere that puts us into a spiritual trance in which all outward consciousness is forgotten. The Vihara also helps us in bringing purity and tranquility to the mind as the spiritual disciplines are practiced there every day. Our children are another important reason to attend the Vihara. We have a responsibility and a commitment to bring them up in the Buddhist way of life. While home training is absolutely important, the Vihara provides an invaluable supplement for the children's spiritual and religious development. In today's society with its drugs, violence, sex, and crime, the most effective way of guiding our children is spiritual training. Attending the Vihara and participating in its activities is a proven way of getting that training.

America will remember their culture, history, and identity. If we have temples, we won't forget our past, we won't lose our culture and traditions. But if we don't have temples, that will be it. Our culture will disappear." In the words of Venerable Maha Ghosananda, a respected Cambodian

A respected elderly monk, the Venerable Balangoda Ananda Maitreya, teaches at Dharma Vijaya Buddhist Vihara, a Sri Lankan temple in Los Angeles. Monks are the religious specialists in the Theravada branch of Buddhism from South and Southeast Asia.

monk from a Rhode Island temple, "If Buddhism survives, then the culture survives."

More than 150 immigrant and refugee temples in the United States now practice the Theravada form of Buddhism found traditionally in Sri Lanka, Myanmar (Burma), Thailand, Laos, and Cambodia. Dharma Vijaya Buddhist Vihara, a Sri Lankan temple established in Los Angeles in 1980, commemorates the Buddha's birth, enlightenment, and final passing away at its annual spring Vesak celebration.

A typical Vesak at Dharma Vijaya spanned an entire weekend, bringing hundreds of Sri Lankans to Dharma Vijaya's modest facility not far from the University of Southern California campus. The property was festooned with bright colors, and flags of the United States and Sri Lanka flew over the fence near the street. Members of the congregation scattered flowers over the Buddha altar in the front room of the temple, eventually burying it under a cloak of blossoms. The men of the congregation constructed a sacred enclosure called a *mandapaya* next to the altar for use in a special ritual to be performed by the Buddhist monks.

A Buddhist Sunday school appreciation program began about 6 P.M. on Saturday. At one point in the proceedings the children recited their school pledge: "My Lord Buddha, until I gain enlightenment I will not violate the sacred precepts, I will not be arrogant before people who are older than myself, I will cherish love in my heart and be a good example to all."

The monks then began an all-night chanting service. Seated in the *mandapaya,* serving in one- to three-hour shifts, they chanted sacred verses called *pirit* that offer protection from harm. At one point during the night a sacred thread was strung around the room for everyone to touch as the monks chanted. At the end of the all-night service, the monks cut this sacred thread into small sections and tied them around the wrists of the congregants as a blessing.

On Sunday morning the temple held a special service for converts to Buddhism, some being new to the faith, some longtime members of Dharma Vijaya. Like many ethnic-Asian temples in America, Dharma Vijaya has welcomed non-Asians seeking knowledge about Buddhism. Special services like this one express the unique status of non-Asian, converted Buddhists within a congregation of Asians born and raised as Buddhists. In some temples, like Dharma Vijaya, "parallel congregations" of Asian and non-Asian Buddhists have formed, each practicing its own form of the religion most of the time, but sometimes gathering for joint activities like the spring celebration of Vesak.

The high point of the weekend's observance came late Sunday morn-

The neon nimbus around the head of the image in the center symbolizes the sacredness of the Buddha for Buddhists. These altars are in Chua Quang Minh, a Vietnamese Buddhist temple in Chicago.

ing as a large crowd gathered to serve the main daily meal to the monks. In Theravada Buddhism this particular interaction has great spiritual significance, because then the monks chant blessings upon the lay people who offer essential gifts of food and other donations to the monks. After everyone had eaten, they all gathered before the Buddha altar in the temple to hear a sermon by one of the monks. Such sermons offer discourses on the Buddha's teachings, often stressing the virtues of wisdom and compassion.

Asian Buddhists living in the United States continue to face prejudice today because of their minority religious and ethnic identities, although extreme forms of violence and open acts of discrimination have been fewer recently than in earlier periods of U.S. history. Many Americans still consider Asians to be strangers in their midst. One interesting measure of prejudice toward specific ethnic groups, first tested by sociologist Emory Bogardus in the 1920s, shows that mainstream Americans have had negative feelings about Asians for many decades. No Asian group has ever scored higher than 19th out of 30 ethnic groups on the so-called Bogardus social distance scale, including the most recent testing in the 1990s. This means that respondents to the Bogardus survey have always rated at least 18 other ethnic groups (mostly Euro-American) more favorably than any Asian group.

"No matter how long you are here in America," remarked Kimmakone Siharath, a Laotian refugee living in southern California, "you will always be an Asian, always an outsider, not an American." Their shared experience as minority Americans, whether Buddhist, Christian, Muslim, or any other religion, has brought many Asian groups together. After the annual Asian American Youth Organization conference in Chicago in 1997, for example, one Thai participant described the activities he had attended. "The workshops were very informative," reported Ben Sriaroon, "and helped us to see the many difficulties our ancestors had, and some of the difficulties today. . . . The racism workshop taught me about how ignorance and racism have made a hard life for Asians today."

Ethnic-Asian Buddhist temples still experience hostility at times. The film *Blue Collar and Buddha* documents the anger felt toward a Laotian temple in Rockford, Illinois, by townspeople who were upset both by lingering feelings about the Vietnam War and high unemployment levels in the 1980s. Other temples report incidents of vandalism and racial name-calling. Opponents sometimes try to block the opening of Buddhist temples in their communities through legal measures such as zoning restrictions. Construction of the Hsi Lai Temple, the large Chinese complex in Hacienda Heights, near Los Angeles, was delayed for years by such opposition.

"Zoning is often used as a thinly veiled way of exerting prejudice," says Chrys Thorsen of the Buddhist Sangha Council of Southern California, an umbrella organization established in 1980 to represent several local Buddhist groups. Similar Buddhist associations have formed elsewhere. Sometimes they serve as watchdogs, protesting what they see as prejudice or discrimination against Buddhism. For example, when a member of the Buddhist Council of the Midwest, established in 1987, was offended by the content of a Saturday morning cartoon show, the Council asked a local television station to supply a videotape of the show to determine whether it contained a racist or offensive portrayal of Asian people and Buddhist monks.

Recent immigrant Buddhists face the same challenges that earlier groups encountered during Americanization. Tensions and compromises arise as communities balance their particular traditional Asian heritage with new American ways. A Cambodian-American insurance representative once spoke of the difficulties of maintaining his religious identity as a Buddhist in America. "I think it is hard to be a good Buddhist in this country," he said, "because from day one we are . . . thrown into a very competitive situation. You have to be number one, you have to be the winner in order to make it in this country. . . . Over here number one is the name of the game, and they don't take number two."

Buddhist temples often take an active role in smoothing the transition from "Asian" to "Asian American" identity for their members. Wat Lao Phouthavong in Catlett, Virginia, for instance, sponsors an annual Fourth of July festival to celebrate both American Independence Day and the religious freedom America offers to Buddhist immigrants and refugees. In 1997 the festival drew nearly 10,000 people, including Burmese, Cambodians, Chinese, Thais, and Vietnamese, as well as Laotians.

Wat Buddhikakhemararama serves the huge Cambodian population in Long Beach, California, offering traditional religious and other cultural events, English as a second language (ESL) classes, and activities for Cambodian children and youth. Boys and men from the community often live as temporary monks in the temple in order to learn the beliefs and practices of Theravada Buddhism, including living without worldly possessions and distractions. In a film documentary titled *Becoming the Buddha in L.A.*, a white U.S. monk named Venerable Benton Pandito is shown giving advice to a Cambodian youth about to be initiated into temporary monkhood. "And later on," Pandito says, "if people ask you, 'What did you get when you became a monk?'—tell them, 'It's not so important that I got anything. It's important what I gave up.'"

The future of ethnic-Asian Buddhism in the United States depends greatly on the willingness of American-born young people like this Cam-

Wat Thai in Los Angeles is decorated for Songkran, the Thai New Year, which takes place in April and includes both Buddhist and Thai cultural activities, sprinkling water on Buddha images and friends, and thoroughly cleaning temples and homes.

bodian youth to carry on the religious heritage of their immigrant and refugee forebears. In the 1930s and 1940s the Nisei or second generation of Japanese-American Buddhists took over the leadership in local temples and national organizations. Today the second generation of recently

Wisa Supanavongs's page in the Thai Youth Club "Graduation '98" booklet. Supanavong, a member of Chicago's Wat Dhammaram, served as the club's president.

Graduation Night' 98   15

DOW

วิสาข์ สุภัณวงศ์   *Wisa Supanavongs*

Parents :   เฉลิมเกียรติ–แสงจันทร์ สุภัณวงศ์

School :   *Alan B Shepard High School*

College :   *University of Illinois (Champaign–Urbana)*

Goals :   *Graduate with a business degree. Travel all over.*

Future :   *Finish College & have a good career & family*

Quote :   *There is a light of the end of each path choose*
                  the right one and it will lead you to your dreans

arrived Buddhist groups stands at a similar point. Perhaps the future can be seen in the words of Wisa Supanavongs, president of the Thai Youth Club at Wat Dhammaram of Chicago. For a graduation-day celebration in 1998 she wrote:

> We know what we've got to do, and we do it because we want to. We don't have to do anything, but what we want to do is to serve our temple in the only ways we know how, which is to pay respect to the Buddha and his teachings, to respect the adults and their wishes (although sometimes they can be a bit outlandish), [to] take care of the temple as if it were our home, and to take care of the younger generations in hopes that they too will see what we teenagers of Wat Dhammaram realize now. And what do we realize now? What we realize is that the temple is not [just] a place of worship, but a place where we have made lifetime friends. . . . We will always come back to it because at one time or another, it was our second home.

Buddhist delegates traveled thousands of miles from their Asian homelands to attend the World's Parliament of Religions held in Chicago in 1893. When a 1993 parliament in the same city commemorated the centennial of that historic first gathering, tens of thousands of Asian-American Buddhists called Chicago home, and many other non-Asian Chicagoans considered Buddhism their religion of choice.

As the 20th century came to a close, one estimate placed the number of Buddhist Americans at 3 million. An umbrella Buddhist organization listed 2,000 groups in its national database. Books about Buddhism sold well, while Internet sites and other new sources of information about Buddhism became ever more numerous. The average American heard more about Buddhism than ever before, and ethnic-Asian Buddhists could no longer be considered newcomers to the United States, having first arrived more than a century and a half earlier.

Chapter 4

Hindus Come to America

Arvind Mehta graduated with top scores in chemical engineering from the Indian Institute of Technology in Bombay, now called Mumbai, in the early 1970s. By that time, he had already received a job offer from a company in Houston, Texas. Mehta traveled by train to Bombay to apply at the U.S. consulate for a visa for permanent resident status in the United States and for the coveted "green card" that would permit him to live and work there legally. With official school records and the formal job offer letters in his briefcase, he entered the building nervously for his interview with the consular officer. He considered this the most important conversation of his life, because it would open or close the door to all the opportunities that America promises to immigrants.

Mehta returned to his home village to await the decision. In the meantime, his parents selected a girl from a neighboring village to be his wife. Just before the wedding, he received the good word from the consulate, and the family celebrated his future prospects by holding an elaborate wedding for more than a thousand guests. Shortly afterward, he left his bride with his parents to await her visa and flew to New York to register as an immigrant. From there he traveled on to Houston to settle in to his new job and make arrangements for his wife to follow him.

Women walk in procession to celebrate the opening of a Hindu temple in Chicago. Carrying decorated water pots and coconuts on their heads is a sign of an auspicious occasion. Those behind perform a joyous Gujarati stick dance.

Five years later, Mehta had achieved considerable success. His wife had joined him, and they had two children, who had automatically become Americans by being born in the United States. He had worked hard to earn significant salary raises and two promotions. He and a few other immigrants from India had organized a monthly meeting of other such families to watch films from home and enjoy meals together. Because he had already decided that he and his family would not return to India, Mehta took advantage of the option offered by the United States, and not by many other countries, for legal immigrants to apply for citizenship. He stood before a judge in the company of immigrants from many countries to be made a U.S. citizen and pledge allegiance to his new homeland.

Arvind Mehta was part of what has become known as the brain drain, the flow of scientists, engineers, physicians, and other professionals from developing countries after the United States passed a new, more open immigration law in 1965. Other immigrants had come to the United States from India before Mehta, although their experiences were quite different from his. Among both the early immigrants and the more recent arrivals, some have shared the experience of being Hindus in America—members of a religion that predominates in India but is a minority faith in the United States.

Before 1965, fewer than 15,000 people from the Indian subcontinent had emigrated to the United States. These included farmers from the Punjab region of northwestern India who, in the late 19th and early 20th centuries, moved to British Columbia, in Canada, and then south into the states of Washington and Oregon. Later they moved still farther south, into California, to escape the aftermath of demonstrations against Asian laborers in Bellingham, Washington, and Vancouver, British Columbia, in September 1907.

In 1923, the U.S. Supreme Court denied these immigrants the opportunity to become citizens. Up to that time, South Asians had been treated as members of the Caucasian, or white, race. But when an Indian man named Bhagat Singh Thind tried to become a U.S. citizen, the Supreme Court ruled, in *United States* v. *Bhagat Singh Thind,* that he and other

South Asians were not "free white persons" under the law. This meant that they could not become U.S. citizens, because a 1790 federal law declared that only white immigrants could apply for naturalized citizenship. After the Thind decision, U.S. immigration and naturalization procedures defined people from India as Asians. The following year, the Immigration Act of 1924 excluded immigrants from China, Japan, Korea, and India from entering the United States. It placed the first permanent limits on immigration and established a "national origins" quota system. The door was effectively closed to Asians and other non-Europeans.

Between 1925 and 1965, many fewer people immigrated to the United States than before or since. In some of these years, in fact, more people left the United States than entered it as immigrants—an unusual situation for a nation of immigrants. Restrictive U.S. immigration laws were one reason for the lull. Other factors were a worldwide economic crisis in the 1920s that made finding work difficult, the Great Depression of the 1930s, and World War II, which disrupted international travel by civilians.

Twenty years after the war ended in 1945, the doors for immigration were reopened by a new law, the Immigration Act of 1965. In the late 19th and early 20th centuries, the Statue of Liberty in New York Harbor had welcomed large numbers of Protestant, Catholic, and Jewish immigrants as they arrived alongside it on ships from Europe. After 1965 it welcomed new immigrants from India and other parts of Asia as they flew in above it on planes that landed at John F. Kennedy Airport. This was fitting, because it was President Kennedy who had proposed the significant changes in U.S. law that had permitted the new immigration. Congress enacted the new immigration law two years after Kennedy's assassination, and President Lyndon B. Johnson signed it into law at a ceremony at the foot of the Statue of Liberty.

The 1965 immigration law admitted Asians and other non-Europeans to the country on an equal basis with Europeans. It did favor some immigrants over others, however, by offering permanent resident status, the first step toward U.S. citizenship, to highly educated and talented people. These new immigrants were not "Your tired, your poor / Your huddled masses yearning to breathe free," in the words of the poet

President Lyndon Baines Johnson signed the Immigration Bill of 1965 on Ellis Island. Unlike the "tired" and "poor" immigrants greeted by the Statue of Liberty earlier in the 20th century, most new immigrants were trained professionals.

Emma Lazarus inscribed on the Statue of Liberty to describe earlier immigrants. Rather, they were professional people—the physicians, engineers, scientists, nurses, and computer specialists needed in the growing U.S. economy. Between 1961 and 1998, some 23 million legal immigrants entered the United States. Almost three-quarters of a million of them came from India.

People from India were numerous and visible among the new immigrants. The 1980 U.S. census counted 387,223 "Asian Indians," permanent residents of the country whose families were from India. Most were graduate students who stayed on to take jobs after completing their studies, or young professionals who had been educated in India or England before accepting jobs in the United States. The immigration law contained provisions for family reunification that allowed their family members to come to the United States, and many did so. The number of Asian Indians doubled to more than 800,000 between 1980 and 1990 and then doubled again in one decade to number almost 1.7 million in the 2000 census. Between 1991 and 1998, over a quarter million new immigrants arrived from India. As a group, Asian Indians are now generally young, well educated, and successful, although some relatives entering for family reunification are not as well prepared or successful. Today the children of the immigrants are attending schools and universities. Some are ready to begin raising the third generation of Asian Indians in the United States since the new round of immigration began in 1965.

Dr. K. C. Patel was one of the new immigrants. Born in 1934 in the state of Gujarat in India, he received his early education in India and then gained admission to the University of Surrey in England, where he received a Ph.D. in chemistry. In 1969 he accepted an invitation to join the chemistry faculty of Brooklyn College in New York City. Three years later his wife and three sons joined him in nearby Flushing, New York.

Although Patel was pleased to be living in the United States, his Hindu faith and heritage remained part of his life. He established a temple of his Hindu tradition, the Bochasanwasi Swaminarayan Satsang (*satsang* means organization), in the basement of his home. In 1971 he became the first national president of that Hindu group, and in the years that followed he guided the group's growth to more than 50,000 members. In 1988 Patel took early retirement from Brooklyn College to volunteer his full-time service to the Swaminarayan group. Like many other Asian Indians, Patel had invested in small businesses such as motels, becoming part owner of a chain of motels in the Southeast. His success in teaching and in business, he claims, provides the freedom so that he can contribute his time to spiritual work.

Around the world, people are migrating to urban centers and to technologically advanced countries. The Asian Indians coming to the United States are part of this global movement. However, because of the preference given to professional people by U.S. immigration law, the Asian Indians in America are a distinct group, with a higher proportion of educated and skilled individuals than Indian populations elsewhere in the world. Nor do they come uniformly from all the states or language groups of India. Gujaratis, from the far western state of Gujarat, make up approximately 40 percent of the immigrants, followed by Punjabis from this northwestern state bordering Pakistan, Hindi speakers from north and central India, Malayalam-speaking Keralites, Tamils and Telugus from the south, and Bengalis from the northeast. On the one hand, Asian Indians in the United States represent a narrow economic and professional segment of the overall Indian population. On the other, however, they represent a wide range of Indian regions and cultures. Their religions include Jainism, Sikhism, and various traditions of Hinduism. These religions are becoming part of the evolving American "gorgeous mosaic" of ethnicities, in the phrase of one New York City mayor.

The Indian subcontinent was the birthplace of several religions: Buddhism, Sikhism, Hinduism, and Jainism, which is closely related to Hinduism. Religions from outside the subcontinent, such as Zoroastrianism (a pre-Islamic faith from Iran), Judaism, Christianity, and Islam, have also attracted followers there. India, like the United States, is a democracy that officially promises freedom of religion, and the subcontinent has nourished a diversity of religious belief and practice. Immigrants from India have brought several forms of religion into greater prominence in the United States. Among these immigrants are Gujarati Jains, many of them from Bombay; Parsis (a name for Zoroastrians in India) from Bombay; Muslims from the north; Christians from the south; and Jews from Kerala's Cochin as well as Bombay. And there are Hindus from all over India.

Hindus make up more than 80 percent of the population of India. Since 1957 official U.S. government records do not identify people by religion, but informal estimates suggest that at the beginning of the 21st century more than a million Americans were Hindus. Despite their many ties to the religions of India, these Americans are creating new forms of their religions in the United States.

Hinduism is a family of religious traditions, each with its own scriptures, leaders, symbols, and social location. Some scholars question whether Hinduism is one religion or many. The word "Hindu" originally referred to the peoples and cultures east of the Indus River in what is now India. It then came to be used to distinguish the native religious and cultural practices of India from those of the Muslims who entered the Indian subcontinent and attracted many converts to Islam. During the British colonial period in India, which ended in 1947, scholars developed a more unified interpretation of the diverse religious beliefs and practices of Hinduism. Some of them have suggested that the railway and telegraph introduced during the colonial period unified India for the first time and led to seeing Hinduism as a nationwide phenomenon. Rapid modern travel and communication have reinforced this concept of Hinduism as a unified entity. As increased contact continues to mold an all-India general agreement about the essentials of Hinduism, the beliefs, practices, festivals, and sacred texts of various regions or sects continue to be absorbed into the general picture of Hinduism.

Perhaps the world's best-known Hindu, Mohandas K. (Mahatma, or Great Soul) Gandhi, called the father of independent India because he led the resistance to British rule that brought Indian independence in 1947, was a Gujarati Hindu who used very effectively methods of peaceful, nonviolent resistance against the British. In March and April 1930 he led a peaceful march to the sea to make salt from sea water, thereby breaking what he believed to be an unjust law giving the British a monopoly on salt production. Thousands joined in the protest, and Gandhi was jailed. Martin Luther King, Jr., and others adapted this strategy of nonviolence to the U.S. civil rights movement in the 1950s and 1960s.

Nevertheless, nonviolence is only one aspect of Hinduism. Hindus worship god in several different forms that are related to two important deities, Vishnu and Shiva, so the main temples are either designated Vaishnava or Shaivite. These two deities between them create and sustain the world. Hindus offer devotion and offerings to them at shrines in their homes and temples. They conduct their lives under religious codes that outline the appropriate conduct for men and women at various stages of life. Hindus' religious calendar has several holy days that are observed with special rituals and visits to the temples. Hindus believe that people are reborn several times, with the circumstances into which they are reborn being determined by how well they performed their duties in their previous existence. Their ultimate goal is release from the cycle of birth, death, and rebirth. Hindus respect holy men and women who have given up worldly concerns, remained unmarried, and devoted themselves to religious service like monks and nuns. They also honor their parents and religious teachers, as one young person said, "like gods"; it is not uncommon to see young Hindus kneel down to touch their parents' feet as a mark of great respect.

Most Hindus in India, however, are not "Hindus in general," even though their religious lives share many common characteristics. They are instead "Hindus in particular," followers of specific varieties of Hinduism. Just as members of other religions are not simply Christians, Buddhists, or Muslims but have other identities such as Arab Muslims, Irish Catholic Christians, or Zen Buddhists, Hindus have many forms of belief and practice. These varying forms, sometimes called *sampradaya* (religious path), create great complexity within Hinduism.

Some followers' paths are determined by language, others by leadership. India has many languages and dialects, generally associated with states and regions. (In the major cities, people from various parts of India typically communicate in English.) Hindus who speak Hindi in the north, Tamil in the south, Bengali in the northeast, or Gujarati in the west represent regional forms of Hinduism. Religious teachers called *gurus* or *acharyas* have significant roles in Hinduism, and the disciples of such teachers follow the path set forth by that teacher. The dividing line between human and divine is relatively thin in many forms of Hinduism, and respected and saintly teachers receive honors similar to those given to the gods. Hindus worship many gods that have multiple names. Vishnu, for example, is also called Venkatesvara and Balaji. The gods appear in various forms in different locations and for diverse purposes. Vishnu appeared as Rama and as Krishna at different times. No single summary of Hinduism is adequate to describe Hindus all over India.

Hinduism is so complex and diverse that it might seem that each Hindu practices his or her own religion, but this is not the case. An individual's social position determines to a large extent the deity, teacher, temple, texts, and festivals central to his or her experience of Hinduism. Each person's religion is shaped by the beliefs and practices of the primary social groups to which he or she belongs—family first of all, then out in broadening circles to best friends, classmates, and peers. An old proverb says, "You choose your gods when you choose your friends."

Immigrants bring with them many of their local traditions from India, but they are also forced to create new expressions of cultural and religious life that are distinctly American. Although they have family backgrounds in various local forms of Hinduism, they often do not recognize themselves in the common descriptions that U.S. schools and media apply to Hindus. They are constantly interacting with powerful forces in U.S. culture that are trying to stamp them into new shapes.

American Hinduism is distinctive, identifiably Hindu, but unlike its forms found elsewhere in the world. American society, custom, and law are affecting Hinduism in certain ways, just as they have affected other religions. For example, religious organizations in the United States must

administer themselves according to certain laws in order to register as tax-exempt organizations. They must have administrative officers, constitutions, bylaws, and trustees, for instance. Hindu immigrants commonly say that they are more active religiously in the United States than they were in India. Many came as young adults directly from university studies in the sciences, an environment in which people are not expected to be very religious. However, their higher level of religious commitment in the United States is striking. It reflects religion's power to provide a strong foundation for personal and group identity in the midst of the enormous transitions of immigration and settling in a new land. Migration is enormously disruptive. It threatens people's traditional concepts and commonly accepted ways of doing things. Immigrants turn to reli-

This illustration from an 1851 encyclopedia includes images of the Hindu triad Brahma (the creator), Vishnu (the preserver), and Shiva (the god of destruction and regeneration).

71

gious and social organizations, not to keep themselves separate from the larger society but to gain a breathing space in which to establish new beliefs and customs that will be effective for themselves and their children in their new homes.

Even though most Hindu immigrants are fluent in English as a legacy of British influence in India, they yearn to speak the Gujarati, Hindi, Tamil, or Telugu languages of their homelands. Religious meetings are one of the few places where immigrants can be "at home" outside their homes. There they can speak their birth language, enjoy the customs of their native place, participate in Indian music, drama, and arts, taste traditional food, and exercise Indian leadership skills in oratory and negotiation. They can discuss how they and their children can best meet the challenges of making a new home and new identities in America. Yet the new Hindu immigrants are not the only ones from South Asia to face such challenges, although they are by far the most numerous.

When newcomers from India arrived in the United States after the Immigration Act of 1965 opened the door, they were surprised to discover some Hindus already present in the U.S. population. Soon they learned about the earlier influence of Hinduism on American culture.

"Missionary Hinduism" is the term scholars have coined to refer to a thread of intellectual Hinduism woven into American society since the mid-19th century. The term also covers forms of Hindu practice adopted by non-Asians in the United States and other countries in the 1960s and afterward. The Hare Krishna movement, which celebrates the Hindu god Krishna, is one such practice. Missionary Hinduism gained attention as a rebellion against aspects of "the American way of life," but it has had little effect on the national culture or religious life in general. The growth of immigrant Hinduism since 1965, on the other hand, is becoming a significant strand in the American multicultural tapestry. As the years go by, however, missionary and immigrant Hinduism are becoming more similar in some ways.

Missionary Hinduism got its start early in the 19th century. A group of intellectuals who came to be called the New England Transcendentalists were attracted to aspects of Hindu philosophy and religion through the writings of Rammohon Roy, a Hindu philosopher and reformer in Bengal, eastern India. As an undergraduate at Harvard University, the writer and philosopher Ralph Waldo Emerson read some sacred texts of Hinduism. He introduced Henry David Thoreau to these texts, which provided material for some of Thoreau's reflections and writings at Walden Pond, including the book *Walden,* suggesting a way of viewing the harmony of humans with nature. The Transcendentalists believed that behind all religions lay a universal human attraction toward a sacred reality. The Hindu teaching that all things, including nature and the material world, are contained in one overarching or transcendent reality called Brahman was attractive to them.

Visitors and teachers from India also spread Hindu teaching to interested American intellectuals. The best-known of these Hindu missionaries was Swami (religious teacher, monk) Vivekananda, who traveled to the World's Parliament of Religions at the Chicago World's Fair in 1893. Newspaper articles praised him, and he became a celebrity as a representative of the "spiritual wisdom of the East," providing an alternative to the "materialism of the West." After the Parliament of Religions, Vivekananda lectured in several U.S. cities and attracted converts to his teaching of Hinduism.

Swami Vivekananda was a leader of the Ramakrishna order of monks in India, which was noted both for its social welfare activities and its religious philosophy, called Vedanta. First taught by Shankara or Śankara, an eighth-century Hindu philosopher, Vedanta is a philosophy of nonduality, or monism. All reality is believed to be united in Brahman. Any apparent distinction between spiritual and physical worlds, humans and gods, humans and other people, humans and the world, or any elements of the material world is an illusion caused by the ignorance of the perceiver. That illusion, or *maya,* is what attaches humans to the cycle of birth, death, and rebirth. According to Vedanta, the true experience of the unity of Brahman cannot be expressed in words, only by not speaking. "Those who speak do not know; those who know do not speak" is a Vedanta saying.

Swami Vivekananda established Vedanta Societies in New York

Hindu students from several schools display a long banner proclaiming Freedom Festival 1997, in celebration of the 50th anniversary of India's independence from Great Britain.

(1894) and San Francisco (1899), bringing Ramakrishna monks from Calcutta to teach Vedanta philosophy and to attract U.S. members. During the 1930s and 1940s, three prominent intellectuals—Aldous Huxley (author of *Brave New World)*, Gerald Heard, and Christopher Isherwood—emigrated to the United States from Britain and revived Vedanta on the West Coast. Membership tripled by the 1950s, then leveled off again. The Vedanta influence continues through some 20 centers and ashrams (places for religious retreats) in the United States. Some Hindu immigrants participate in Vedanta Society activities, and the Ramakrishna monks often lecture at gatherings of Hindu immigrants, but the primary focus of the Vedanta Societies remains on teaching the larger, nonimmigrant society.

During the 1970s, Indian immigrants arriving in U.S. airports were astounded to see young, white Americans dressed in Hindu garb, dancing, chanting praises to the Hindu god Krishna, and passing out Hindu devotional literature. These young people were converts to Krishna devotion and members of the International Society for Krishna Consciousness

(ISKCON), sometimes called the Hare Krishnas, because of their chants of "Hare Krishna, Hare Krishna; Krishna Krishna, Hare Hare."

Abhay Charan De established the movement in 1966. He immigrated from India in 1965, took the title A. C. Bhaktivedanta Swami Prabhupada, and began to preach his form of Hindu devotion to young people in the parks of New York City. By the time of his death in 1977, he had personally initiated 5,000 disciples as worshipers of Krishna and was the chief religious figure for thousands of young American followers who expressed their rejection of family and American values by looking toward Asian spiritual traditions. Some full-time members were celibate, sworn to remain unmarried and to abstain from sexual relations. Others were married with children. Some lived in ISKCON temples and ashrams, performed the daily cycle of rituals in the temple, chanted and sang devotional songs, and publicly proclaimed their Hinduism in airports and on the streets of major cities. Vedanta had attracted Westerners to Indian philosophy and theology, or religious study. ISKCON drew them to the path of intense personal devotion (*bhakti*) to a Hindu deity, Krishna, and to a guru, Swami Prabhupada

ISKCON became popular at a turbulent period of American history when many young people were rebelling against commonly held beliefs and practices. Josh Cohen was a student at an elite midwestern college in the early 1970s when he first met a group of ISKCON devotees. He had become dissatisfied with the lifestyle of his wealthy parents and had experimented with drugs. After a few sessions of chanting and instruction, he took initiation from Swami Prabhupada, dropped out of college, severed ties with his family, and went to live in a Krishna temple at a location kept secret from his parents. For several years Cohen helped spread his group's beliefs and sold ISKCON literature in airports and on city streets. After Prabhupada died in 1977, however, Cohen married a fellow ISKCON member and they left the group, in part because their real loyalty had been to their *guru* and they were dissatisfied with the new leaders. They moved to Tennessee, where Josh found a job as a car salesman and they started a family. Cohen's experience was shared by many of the converts at the same time that Hindu immigrants were exploring ISKCON.

The ISKCON temples attracted some of the early immigrants from India who had not yet established their own temples, and ISKCON members began to act as priests and teachers for some of the immigrant families. The group has established temples and ashrams in several countries, including India, where some converts from Western countries serve as priests and religious specialists. North America is the only region where ISKCON has not shown growth since the death of its founder. Divisions within the group and legal disputes without, including criminal charges against some leaders and lawsuits claiming child abuse in some ISKCON schools, have led to many defections and a decline in membership. Fewer than 2,000 full members are currently associated with ISKCON in the United States.

Several other Hindu teachers also attracted disciples and founded organizations in the United States. Paramhansa Yogananda came to Boston in 1920 to attend a conference sponsored by the Unitarian Church. He remained in the United States and founded the Self-Realization Fellowship in 1920 also. It ultimately gained a reported membership of 200,000 and was the largest Hindu organization in the United States until the 1960s. Siva Yogaswami of India founded the Saiva Siddhanta Church there in 1949 when he ordained a U.S. convert, Sivaya Subramuniyaswami, as his successor. Subramuniyaswami returned to the United States and established a headquarters in Kauai, Hawaii. The Saiva Siddhanta Church publishes a newspaper, *Hinduism Today,* that reports on the growing influence of Hinduism in America.

The line between Hindu religious devotion and new age psychology and meditation is thin. A number of yoga and meditation centers and holistic health programs claim not to be religious but have roots in Hinduism. Among these are ayurvedic diet and medicine, which prescribes foods to be eaten and avoided by people who have certain body types. Yoga originated as a meditation discipline that combined spiritual and physical training. Today it exists in many forms, some more spiritually oriented than others. Many gyms and physical therapists teach yoga as a type of exercise or an aid to relaxing. The most successful popular-culture offshoot of Hinduism is called Transcendental Meditation (TM).

Sisters and Brothers of America

A statue of Swami Vivekananda on the grounds of the Hindu Temple of Greater Chicago commemorates his missionary visit to the World's Parliament of Religions at the Chicago World's Fair in 1893.

Swami Vivekananda represented Hinduism in the World's Parliament of Religions in Chicago in 1893. His manner, dress, and speeches on "the spiritual wisdom of the East" made him a celebrity. Swami Vivekananda became the precursor and model for gurus and teachers of Hinduism in America in the 20th century. In his opening address to the Parliament he calls for tolerance.

Sisters and Brothers of America

It fills my heart with joy unspeakable to rise in response to the warm and cordial welcome which you have given us. I thank you in the name of the most ancient order of monks in the world; I thank you in the name of the mother of religions, and I thank you in the name of millions and millions of Hindu people of all classes and sects.

My thanks, also, to some of the speakers on this platform who, referring to the delegates from the Orient, have told you that these men from far-off nations may well claim the honor of bearing to different lands the idea of toleration. I am proud to belong to a religion which has taught the world both tolerance and universal acceptance. We believe not only in universal toleration, but we accept all religions as true. I am proud to belong to a nation which has sheltered the persecuted and the refugees of all religions and all nations of the earth. . . .

The present convention, which is one of the most august assemblies ever held, is in itself a vindication, a declaration to the world of the wonderful doctrine preached in the Gita: "Whosoever comes to Me, through whatsoever form, I reach him; all men are struggling through paths which in the end lead to me." Sectarianism, bigotry, and its horrible descendant, fanaticism, have long possessed this beautiful earth. They have filled the earth with violence, drenched it often and often with human blood, destroyed civilization and sent whole nations to despair. Had it not been for these horrible demons, human society would be far more advanced than it is now. But their time is come; and I fervently hope that the bell that tolled this morning in honor of this convention may be the death-knell of all fanaticism, of all persecutions with sword or with pen, and of all uncharitable feelings between persons wending their way to the same goal.

An Indian teacher called the Maharishi Mahesh Yogi established it after he arrived in the United States in 1959. Several celebrities, including the Beatles and actress Mia Farrow, were attracted to TM's form of yoga, which lost its religious characteristics and was accepted as a program of stress reduction in the U.S. military and in some public schools.

Some missionary forms of Hinduism have been more short-lived, such as an experiment at Rajneeshpuram, Oregon. This ashram became notorious in the 1980s because of reports that the group's *guru*, Rajneesh, taught and practiced "free love" and other forms of unconventional sexual behavior. He was also widely criticized for his opulent lifestyle, which included owning many expensive Rolls-Royce automobiles. Although the sect originated in Pune, India, Rajneesh established his ashram and headquarters in the small rural community of Antelope, Oregon. Local people became alarmed when he purchased large tracts of land, recruited members from American cities, transported them to Oregon, and registered enough voters to take over the government of the community. Citizens complained that he had established what amounted to a religious dictatorship in which the sect controlled local politics. The ashram disbanded after Rajneesh left the United States under a cloud of negative publicity.

Negative public reaction to some expressions of Hinduism in the United States, especially those involved in making converts among American young people, made it more difficult for Hindu immigrants to gain respect for their religion. Ironically, most of the highly successful immigrants had ways of life and values much more familiar to those of mainstream America than were the

The temple of the Vedanta Society in San Francisco was one of the first American Hindu temples. The Vedanta teachings of Swami Vivekananda attracted a number of western converts to Hindu philosophy.

ideas of the missionary Hindus who cut their ties to their families, favored communal living, and carried out austere lives of self-denial and full-time religious activity.

Today many strands of Hinduism are flowing together in America, some from missionary Hinduism and others swelling with immigration from India. The institutions and influence of the Hindu immigrants, however, have now largely eclipsed missionary Hinduism. These are developing away from the glare of publicity but have more significance than missionary Hinduism for the future of religion in America.

A member of the International Society for Krishna Consciousness sells literature about Krishna in a Cincinnati public square. The sale of literature raises money and spreads the religion.

Chapter 5

Hindus at Home

As Dr. Ravindra Marri left his home in Bangalore, India, to enter a medical residency program at a hospital in New York City, his mother carefully handed him cloth-wrapped religious objects from their home shrine. They included a small image of Ganesh (the deity who protects people from danger and assists students), a copy of the *Bhagavad Gita* (a Hindu religious text), images of Krishna and Radha, a picture of the family's *guru* (religious teacher) in a silver frame, a small oil lamp, and an incense holder. In his New York apartment, Marri placed these objects on a shelf beside the bed. Later he went back to India to get married and returned to New York with his wife. She brought sacred objects from her home and set up a small shrine in the kitchen. They consolidated the sacred objects in a home shrine in the family room of their first house.

Because Hinduism is family oriented and home based, shrines in the home have a significant role. Most Hindu families have such shrines. Some are whole rooms set apart for elaborate shrine cabinets carved in India. Others are as simple as a few pictures of deities and religious teachers on a wall or in a china closet. A considerable amount of Hindu religious life occurs in the home; the traditional marriage ceremony authorizes the husband and wife to perform religious rituals for the family. Indeed, the home shrine is an authentic residence of the gods and the site of most Hindu rituals, so it is possible to be an observant Hindu and

Children pray before a Hindu home shrine set up in a closet of their home in Wooster, Ohio. Family rituals at home are at least as important for Hindus as worship in the temples.

rarely visit a temple. Some scholars say that Hinduism's secure place in domestic life, centered in home shrines and family rituals, is the main reason Hinduism has survived so successfully through the turbulent, centuries-long history of invasions and conquests of the Indian subcontinent. Its home-based strategy has also helped preserve Hinduism through the potentially unsettling process of immigration to the United States.

A home shrine is a statement of Hindu identity for a family, like a crucifix on the wall of a Roman Catholic home or prayer and Bible reading at the dinner table in a Protestant home. The parents' level of devotion determines the intensity of activity at the home shrine. Parents can select from a wide array of religious rituals represented in the various forms of Hinduism, and devotional activities have changed as the immigrant community has moved from the first to the second and then on to the third generation.

The home shrine is the focus for the morning or evening *puja*, which is a ritual of chanting sacred *mantras* (verses or syllables), studying religious texts, meditation, and *arti*, or waving the lighted oil lamp before the sacred images. *Arti* dates from earlier times when shrines were without electric lights. Waving the lamp enabled the individual to see the image and to be seen by the god, which was thought to be the central act of worship. A common practice is for the oldest woman in the household to offer the *puja*, and in many homes the food offered to the family and guests at meals is first dedicated to the gods at the home shrine. As an example of how devotional practices are evolving in the United States, the hectic pace of American life for all family members makes it difficult to set aside time for daily observance. Some immigrants speak about engaging in abbreviated *pujas* and forms of meditation while traveling to their workplaces or schools.

On important occasions when worshipers seek the favor of the gods, such as when moving into a new house or establishing a business, a Brahmin comes to the house to perform a special *Satya Narayan Puja*, a more elaborate *puja* featuring chants of sacred texts, offerings to the gods, and dedications of the parents and the home. Brahmins are members of the highest Indian caste; in the traditional social and religious ranking they are authorized to perform special rituals. In Brahmin households, the father can perform the rituals if he has been appropriately trained by his father, but others hire a Brahmin *pujari,* a priest who serves in a temple, or a Brahmin employed in another occupation who nonetheless knows the rituals and performs them for the Hindu community. Generally, the Brahmin must shorten the ritual and explain elements as he goes along in order to keep the attention of those who attend, especially the children of the second and third generations. At one ritual, for example, the children were surprised when the priests inserted into the traditional list of sacred rivers some familiar names of American rivers, reciting, "the Ganges, the Ohio, the Mississippi, and the Yamuna." A dinner, which makes the event a significant social occasion at which family and friends gather, follows the ceremony. It is common for Hindus in periods of transition from one stage of life to the next to make vows regarding career choices, family security, and the welfare and health of their children. They fulfill these vows by performing religious rituals or sponsoring readings of sacred texts in the home.

Hindus have an elaborate series of 16 rituals to mark transitions, called *samskaras,* which begin before birth and continue after death with cremation and observances of the anniversary of death. Rarely, even in India, do families observe all these rituals. In the United States, the five rituals most often performed are those before birth, the name-giving for a newborn child, the sacred thread ceremony for Brahmin boys, marriage, and cremation.

Each ritual is adapted

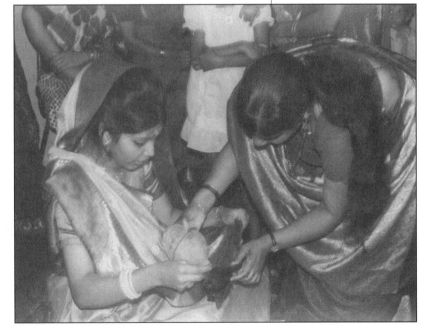

An older married woman with children performs a special *puja* (ritual) in which Gita Patel (left) receives a coconut that has been made sacred, to bless her and her unborn child.

to the American context. For example, rituals performed during pregnancy are traditionally conducted in Sanskrit, a classical language of India and of the earliest Hindu sacred texts. Today, American Hindus announce this ritual in the same way that other Americans announce baby showers, and the rituals have taken on some aspects of the shower. In the same way, a Brahmin priest in the home performs the name-giving ceremony, but the surrounding social activities are similar to those for a Christian baptism. The sacred thread ceremony for a Brahmin boy occurs when he becomes a student. In earlier times in India, the boy would then leave home to live and study with a *guru*. Now the ceremony functions as a puberty ritual similar to a Christian confirmation or a Jewish bar mitzvah. During the ritual the boy receives a sacred thread. Afterward he wears it over his left shoulder as a symbol of his status as a Brahmin. Despite the Americanization of some aspects of the rituals in the United States, in many cases families return to India for some of the childhood rituals and for marriages so that these ceremonies can be performed according to traditional patterns and grandparents and the extended family can participate.

Because marriage marks a major transition of life into householder status, a wedding is the occasion for an elaborate ritual. Arranged marriage is the Indian tradition; many immigrants married their spouses in this way. Their parents selected their marriage partners and arranged the wedding. Hindus often remark that "the expectation in America is that you will marry the person you come to love; in India the expectation is that you will love the one you marry." One young immigrant couple laughed together about their experience. The man returned to India on a two-week vacation to select a bride from among several girls his parents had arranged for him to meet. Before he left New York, he and some friends prepared a list of 10 questions he would ask each girl at their first meeting. But when he set eyes on one girl, he forgot the list because she was so beautiful and nice—and "modern," with her hair cut in a contemporary style. She was modern in her thinking, too; she said that she wanted to marry a pharmacist rather than a physician, because he would have more time for his family. They married, and she joined him in New York after obtaining her visa. They seem to be very happily married.

Because the Western custom of courtship and dating is not part of the traditional pattern in India, many immigrant parents are reluctant to let their children date. They are fearful of the results of romantic entanglements and of possible casual sexual relations. Yet many Hindu children born and raised in the United States resist their parents' subtle attempts to select their spouses. One family solved the problem of prom night by agreeing that their son could go to the prom, but only if they chose the girl he invited. They then talked with her parents to set the ground rules for the evening, which put more emphasis on the evening than either the boy or the girl desired. The evening was a success from the parents' point of view, but both young people were embarrassed and resented what they saw as artificial formality in the arrangement. They considered the date to be a disaster and were glad when it was over.

Conflicts over dating and marriage illustrate a fundamental problem for Hindus in the United States. For parents, the primary emphasis of social relationships is on family and family ties, but for their American children it is on friendship. Dating can create tension, because parents see it as the first step toward starting a family, while young people simply want to enjoy and explore friendships and their feelings for one another. Increasingly, parents in the United States and even in India are agreeing to either "semiarranged marriages," in which the couple express interest in each other and ask their parents to negotiate a marriage, or "love marriages," in which the partners select each other—the pattern that many see as the American norm. It appears that so far, however, the divorce rate for Hindu immigrants is much lower than for the general American population.

A wedding is the Hindu ritual most likely to be witnessed by friends who are not Hindus. The typical ceremony includes a *homa* (fire sacrifice) during which a Brahmin priest pours oil, various grains, and offerings into a sacred fire while chanting the appropriate texts in Sanskrit from the *Vedas,* the most sacred ancient religious texts of India. Many priests now add explanations of the chants in English to help guests understand basic Hindu rituals and symbols. Such additions can point up

A Brahmin priest reads the wedding ceremony in Sanskrit for a couple in traditional wedding dress. A charcoal grill is used for the ritual fire sacrifice.

the differences between tradition and the new circumstances of Hindus in the United States. In the middle of one ceremony, for example, the priest translated from Sanskrit into English the traditional roles of husband as provider and wife as homemaker. Then, looking up, he added wryly, "but now you are in America, so you will do whatever you want." Then he returned to the Sanskrit chant.

Most weddings are too large for homes. They are held in rented halls, with traditional elements sometimes adapted to meet new settings. One priest, for example, had to perform a symbolic *homa* sacrifice over a candle, because the local fire regulations in a Holiday Inn would not permit the full ritual to be carried out over an open fire. The bride generally wears a red *sari*—one long piece of fabric wound intricately around the body—threaded with gold and elaborate gold jewelry. A highlight of the wedding ceremony comes when the groom ties a thread around himself and his bride and they walk around the sacred fire seven times, repeating a traditional vow at each turn regarding food, strength, increasing wealth, good fortune, children, long life, and eternal friendship. Much gift-giving and a large banquet generally accompany wedding ceremonies in both India and the United States.

Marriage moves the couple into the traditional householder stage of life. Accordingly, the priest urges them to establish themselves securely in regard to worldly goods and to provide well for their children. These social obligations will be their responsibility until the children are educated and established in homes of their own. Then, according to the traditional pattern, the parents will enter the third stage of life, gradual separation from the responsibilities of the householder. A few then enter the fourth and final stage, becoming *sannyasin,* people who separate themselves from all worldly attachments to pursue lives of simplicity and spiritual devotion. Few Hindu immigrants in the post-1965 wave have reached retirement age, and only a few parents of immigrants have become permanent residents of the United States. Even fewer have entered the traditional fourth stage and given up all social obligations or ties. However, some immigrants do commit themselves to full-time volunteer service in Hindu temples and organizations following retirement.

Some rituals are concerned with death and mourning. Cremation, now widely practiced in the United States, has long been the traditional Hindu method of disposing of the bodies of the dead. It is clean and consistent with the Hindu belief that although the soul is immortal, the body is not. In India, relatives and friends gather on the day of a death to carry the body to the cremation grounds, where the eldest son ignites the funeral pyre. That practice is neither practical nor permitted in the United States. Some members of the Hindu community have therefore had to master the legal requirements for cremation and for the disposal of the ashes either in the United States or in India. Others have had to learn the appropriate rituals and have even prepared instruction manuals for performing them. It is common for families to take the ashes of the cremated dead to India to be cast into one of the sacred rivers—the Ganges, if at all possible—and for the required memorial rituals.

Hindus view life as moving through numerous stages and cycles, even cycles that reach beyond a single life. They believe in *samsara,* or reincarnation, the idea that at death a person is reborn into another existence. His or her character in that existence is determined by *karma,* or action or activity; the results of all actions affect the soul's entire existence. In each stage of life, one's *dharma* or duty is to do what is right in a particular social situation. *Dharma* is the basis of the ancient law codes of Hinduism and of the basic moral instruction that parents attempt to pass on to their children.

The chants used in these family rituals are from the *Rig Veda,* the most sacred Hindu scripture. This collection of hymns is the world's old-

Hindu Weddings

Indian weddings are the Hindu rituals most often observed by non-Hindu Americans. Priests and families transform the ancient ceremony to serve Hindus in America. A. V. Srinivasan, an engineer who leads Hindu wedding rituals, reflects in this essay on his role in that transformation. He is a leader in the Connecticut Valley Hindu Temple Society.

I have been helping Hindu families in and around Connecticut for over a decade when their sons or daughters plan to marry. . . . Over the years I have been impressed by the genuine interest on the part of the younger generation in understanding Vedic wedding practices and the philosophy behind them. At the same time it has become clear to me that many parents may lack basic knowledge of the practices although they very much relish the fact that their son or daughter wishes to respect their heritage. . . . Parents who married in India 20 or 30 years ago went through the motions in front of their own parents and supporting relatives. . . . No one, least of all the officiating priests, insisted that they understand [the rituals] before they made the most personal commitment in life. It was even considered fashionable to look down on the rituals and consider the event as a social experience!

When young people approach me now asking me to perform their weddings, I am touched by their desire to understand each of the several steps they will be taking during the ceremony and I am happy to oblige. I first make sure that they want a Hindu wedding and are not doing it to please someone else. . . . We have tried to help families by developing a procedure based on scriptures, with necessary variations to suit individual family traditions. Through this effort I have been able to convey to the families that the procedures prescribed by our ancestors are full of meaning and beauty as the scriptures charge the couple with responsibilities they inherit by virtue of the union.

The Hindu wedding ceremony is based on Vedic traditions and rituals originating in the Rig Veda, the earliest of the four ancient Sanskrit books of knowledge which form the basis of Hinduism. Conjugal union has always been considered an important religious celebration, defining the beginning of the third stage of earthly existence, the first two being childhood and student life. These rituals, which date back at least 5,000 years, form a significant dramatic sequence.

est sacred scripture still used in worship today. Although only a few wor-shipers understand the Sanskrit language in which the hymns are written, they value the rhythm and power of the chanting. Hindus in the United States circulate audiocassettes of Vedic chanting, and some chants are available on the Internet.

A young Brahmin named Rajgopal Krishnacharya memorized the Sanskrit verses of the *Vedas* by repeating them with his father every morning at the family *puja* as he was growing up in India. Now he is an engineer living in Oklahoma and is one of the few people there who know the chants. He is often invited to lead rituals in Hindu homes in the area. Some of the chants have slipped from his memory, so he collects copies of the texts that include pronunciations of the Sanskrit words to refresh his memory and make him able to chant correctly.

Hindu homes are more than the primary sites of religious teaching, rituals, and ceremonies. In the years before American Hindus established temples and cultural centers, homes were the gathering places for reli-gious groups. Relatives and friends began to gather in homes once or twice a month on the weekend for worship, study, or meditation. Through these groups, Hindus could pursue the four traditional paths of Hindu practice: *bhakti* (devotion), *yoga* (meditation), *jnana* (knowledge), and *karma* (action).

Devotional groups gather before images of deities or other sacred objects to express their reverence. A common form of expression in devo-tion is to sing sacred hymns and songs in honor of the deity or sacred person. These hymns, or *bhajans*, are in the regional languages of India, such as Gujarati, Hindi, Tamil, Telugu, and Malayalam. They take on a distinct ethnic identity.

Meditation groups focus on the physical, mental, and spiritual disci-plines of *yoga*. They have spread some of the Indian ideas and practices that have significantly influenced American society. However, while many Americans have adopted some elements of Hindu meditation and other Hindu-influenced practices such as vegetarianism, surprisingly few Hindu immigrants practice yoga.

Followers of the *jnana* path meet in homes to engage in detailed study of Hindu religious texts. Study groups called *Gita mandals* (*mandals* meaning "society") have met in homes for years to study the *Bhagavad Gita*, the best-loved and best-known Hindu religious text. It consists of a philosophical and devotional dialogue between a warrior named Arjuna and his charioteer, who is really the god Krishna. The poetic dialogue takes place on a battlefield just before a battle between two royal families. It contains Hinduism's basic teachings about the gods, duty, devotion, and many other aspects of the Hindu worldview. The *Gita* has become a religious classic because, over the centuries, teachers have been able to interpret its enigmatic verses in ways that are meaningful to Hindus living in many times and places. Now they are applying its lessons to the new and different lives that Hindus are leading in the United States.

The *Upanishads* are poetic verses added to the *Vedas*. Enigmatic sayings that embody wisdom, they have inspired Hindu philosophers such as Shankara in the 8th century, Ramanuja in the 12th century, and Mahatma Gandhi, the religious and political leader of India's 20th-century struggle for independence. Philosophically inclined Hindus gather for study sessions to interpret verses of the *Upanishads* and examine the lessons of previous interpreters.

In the early days, all these study groups had leaders who worked at secular occupations, with only minimal formal instruction in Hindu thought and practice. They typically possessed excellent organizational skills that supported the growth and success of the study groups, but they needed help interpreting the texts. Thus they viewed videotapes of lectures by scholars and teachers from India, discussed the lectures, and eventually began inviting some of these teachers to come to the United States for summer-long tours to lecture on the sacred texts. For larger gatherings they sponsored meetings in schools, park district halls, and church social halls. Each summer now brings more and more *gurus* and teachers for lecture tours across the United States.

The paths of devotion, meditation, and study are not mutually exclusive, and Hindus generally forge creative combinations of all three as they attempt to create a style of worship and religious practice appropriate to their new homeland and surroundings. Hindu immigrants also grapple with the age-old question: What is the better way to preserve religious traditions and transmit them to one's children, through ritual or word? Is it better to follow traditional rituals using the sacred Sanskrit language and the gestures that have always accompanied the language? Perhaps the beauty and power of the repeated chants and actions will attract the loyalty and allegiance both of immigrants and their children. Or is it better to rely on words to communicate, interpreting the sacred teachings to give children a clear understanding of the intellectual foundation of their beliefs and practices? Perhaps transmitting basic teachings to children and grandchildren, usually in English, will establish the foundation of a truly American Hinduism. One form of communication that offers a compromise is visual presentation of sacred Hindu stories through acting and reciting.

Several sacred texts lend themselves well to performance, spoken recitation, and teaching. Two ancient epics are particularly popular in both India and the United States. The *Ramayana* is the story of good King Rama, whose beautiful wife, Sita, is kidnapped by evil King Ravana. (Rama is a Hindu god, and Sita is his companion goddess.) In the long search for Sita, Rama is aided by his brother, Lakshmana, and by Hanuman, the king of the monkeys. Finally, after many heroic deeds and much soul-searching, they rescue Sita from the island of Sri Lanka, off the southeastern coast of India. The story has long been popular not only in India but throughout Southeast Asia and in other countries where Hindus have carried their culture. A dramatization of the *Ramayana* shown as a serial on the Indian government television network over several weeks became the most popular television show in India. Throughout the United States, Indian video outlets and grocery stores distribute copies of

Young people display a poster supporting vegetarianism. Many Hindus and Jains avoid killing or injuring any animal and, like Mahatma Gandhi, practice nonviolence.

this show. Hindus watch them as entertainment in their homes and as teaching in religious gatherings.

The other popular ancient epic is the *Mahabharata,* the story of a great war between two clans of cousins, the good Pandavas and the bad Kauravas. The complex story of the Pandavas' effort to regain territory they lost to the Kauravas is the world's longest epic poem, complete with exciting tales, theological reflections, intrigue, a long love story, examples of moral behavior, and philosophical musings. The *Bhagavad Gita* is only a small section of the *Mahabharata,* inserted into the long story at the point of the decisive battle. Arjuna, the hero of the Pandavas, sees his cousins arrayed on the opposite side of the battlefield, throws his bow and arrows to the side, and sits down in his chariot. The question that begins the dialogue with Krishna is whether he should enter into battle and kill his cousins. The surprising answer leads to a long discussion about duty, the goals of life, and the role of faithfulness and devotion in gaining liberation from the cycles of birth and death. Like the *Ramayana,* the *Mahabharata* was made into a long-running series on Indian television.

Videotapes are used to retell the story in America. In addition, young people use dance and dramatic acting to perform episodes from both stories at religious and cultural gatherings. Other Hindu sacred texts, called *puranas,* contain the stories of the Hindu gods. Some are in Sanskrit and are accepted as sacred texts by all Hindus. Other texts, most of them in the more widely used regional languages, come from the subdivisions of Hinduism and are used only by Hindus who worship a particular deity or follow a certain saint or *guru.* Some Gujarati texts, for example, recount stories popular among Swaminarayan Hinduism.

Vinod Patel is one such Hindu. He is the son of Gujarati parents who are devoted followers of Swaminarayan Hinduism. They carefully taught him Gujarati so that he could read the sacred texts. Later, as a university premedical student, he often lectured on the *Vachanamritam* at weekly meetings held in his parents' home. The *Vachanamritam* is a series of sermons given by the reformer Swaminarayan at the beginning of the 19th century. Swaminarayan attracted a group of followers, established temples in the state of Gujarat, and came to be worshiped as the manifestation of the highest divinity. Vinod Patel's father, who is the coordinator of the group in their city, at meetings often chants Sanskrit verses of the *Shikshaptri,* a collection of the rules of conduct that Swaminarayan prescribed for his followers. They call for a strict discipline of self-control, avoiding attachment to worldly pleasures, and nonviolence in word and deed. Another favorite text is the *Satsangijivan,* which recounts stories about Swaminarayan. Accounts of his parents, birth, activities as a child, travels around India as a poor monk, and leadership of a growing group of followers in Gujarat provide many illustrations and points of discussion for sermons and lectures. Each subgroup within Hinduism, like the followers of Swaminarayan, has its own constellation of sacred texts and stories.

Immigrant parents are often anxious to start religious groups when their children become old enough to enter school and begin to be shaped by influences outside the home. At that time the parents tend to seek people from the same religious tradition to help them raise their children in ways that will preserve their values, identity, and relationships with their Hindu heritage. Groups of Hindu parents in several cities have started Sunday schools similar to those in Christian churches in order to teach their children the basics of Hinduism and Indian culture. These met at first in homes, then in rented halls or in the cultural centers that sprang up when the Asian Indian community grew large enough to support

Members of the Abhinaya Dance Company perform a scene from the Hindu epic the *Mahabharata.* Stories from the *Mahabharata* told through drama, dance, song, film, and art help immigrants and their children remember their roots.

them. At these Sunday schools, children learned the basic rituals, religious stories and teachings, and symbolic religious art and drama.

Summer camps and retreats for children and young people supplement the Sunday schools. These camps are intended to help parents convey Hinduism to their children and, in doing so, to preserve, protect, and pass on the spiritual heritage of India. One of the first summer camps was held in the Pocono Mountains at a retreat center led by an American woman who converted to Hinduism and became a religious teacher for families of immigrants. Another way Hindu parents can attempt to immerse their children in their religion and in Indian culture is to take or send them back to India for visits to relatives and sacred shrines and for instruction by religious leaders. Hindus in India commonly go on pilgrimages to noted temples, such as the Krishna temple at Dwarka in Gujarat or the Venkateswara temple in Andhra Pradesh, in the southeast. They also visit sacred sites, such as the Ganges River, or holy persons. Visits to India by American Hindus take on aspects of sacred pilgrimages. Religious groups organize some tours, but families privately conduct most visits.

Children roast marshmallows at a Hindu Heritage summer camp. Several Hindu summer camp programs provide instruction in the religion, as well as in the history, culture, and languages of India.

As children of the second generation reach college age, they begin to learn about Hinduism and Indian culture in courses at colleges and universities. In previous decades these courses existed to teach U.S. college students about distant cultures and religions. Now an increasing number of students in the courses are Hindus who want to learn more about their own religion. One reason the function of the courses has changed in recent years is that the affluent immigrant community has been active in raising funds for programs in Indian studies at major universities such as Columbia, the University of California at Santa Barbara, and Indiana University.

The family remains, however, the primary vehicle through which Hindu traditions pass from one generation to the next. It is also the setting within which individuals form their own religious identities. In the United States, Hindu families must meet these responsibilities without the wide support network that exists in Indian society. And it is hard. One mother remarked, "Here I have to be priest and preacher, and it doesn't work."

Many parents say that they have found themselves to be more religious in the United States than they were in India, partly because they have to organize all religious functions themselves and to provide all religious instruction for their children. When speaking about themselves, the immigrants describe the purpose of religious activities as "to gain peace," "to show devotion to God," and "to gain God's blessing." When they speak about the purpose of religion for their children and grandchildren, they respond, "so they will know who they are," "so they will not get lost in American society," and "so my son will have the best of both cultures."

Chapter 6

Hindu Temples

H undreds of Hindus gathered for the dedication of a new Hindu temple at Lemont, Illinois, near Chicago, in January 1985. Brahmin priests from India had spent the previous days performing the ancient rituals to prepare the site and install the images of the gods in their new home. At the most favorable moment, the people carried the metal images around the outside of the temple, preceded by Brahmins chanting Sanskrit verses. Large, elaborately decorated umbrellas protected the sacred images of Rama, Sita, Lakshmana, and Hanuman. The crowd, dressed in colorful traditional clothing, followed the images. Each woman carried a water pot with a coconut and flowers covering it, a sign of an especially significant occasion. They followed the images through the temple doors, shouting praises to Rama, the main deity of the temple.

Inside the temple shrines, priests carefully followed the ancient rituals that change the large granite statues carved from dead blocks of stone into representations of the living presence of the deities. They purified the images with water, milk, and honey, then decorated them with colorful garments and valuable ornaments. In the central act, the priest put his hand on the chest of each image and chanted the verse that invoked the breath of life and a divine presence in the image. Finally, the priest "opened the eyes" of the image with a golden needle so the deity could "see" the world. The first gaze of the deity is very powerful and is thus

Hindu priests perform a *homa* ritual, that is, burning offerings such as rice and other grains. Fire sacrifices accompany many auspicious occasions, such as the dedication of a temple or the initiation of Hindu monks.

A Brahmin priest performs preliminary rites preparing images of deities to be placed in the shrine of a new Hindu temple. Hindu temples normally house many images of deities.

supposed to fall upon something favorable or at least neutral, because if it were to fall upon something negative its power might destroy the world. To avert disaster, the priest holds a mirror before the face of the image, so that its gaze will fall upon its own reflection. In some cases, it is said, the mirror cracks before the intense power of the gaze. To complete the consecration of the temple, a modern crane lifted the priests above the elaborately carved tower. Directly above the deity, they poured water and flowers over the tower, chanted the appropriate Sanskrit verses, and "opened the eye" of the temple to establish the link between earth and heaven. A helicopter then flew over the temple scattering rose petals.

Once these rituals have been performed, the deities at a new temple are ready to welcome their devotees daily to have *darshan*, or "seeing." In the morning, priests prepare the deities for visits by their devotees and present them with gifts and offerings. Priests perform a daily round of rituals to awaken, bathe, feed, and dress the deities in preparation for visits. Afterward, the deities "give *darshan*" and devotees "have *darshan*" of the deities. This is the highest act of devotion for Hindus. Preparation includes a ritual purification in a full bath or a symbolic sprinkling with water, removing one's shoes, walking around the shrine with one's right side (thought to be purer than the left) toward the deity, and, perhaps, chanting Sanskrit texts or singing songs in praise of the deity. Inside the shrine, the priest performs *arti,* the waving of a lamp before the deity.

Temples are open throughout the day, but many Hindus in the United States live at some distance from their temples and may attend only on weekends and for special festivals. Temples in the United States are of many different types. The architecture may be Western or Indian. Some temples are grand, others humble. They may house many deities or only a few, and they may employ many full-time priests and other employees or be served by volunteers.

The experiences of five friends at a suburban high school near Chicago illustrate the different roles that temples play in the lives of American Hindu families. The five young people regularly visit four different temples; they also discuss starting a Hindu Club and visiting all the Chicago temples.

Girish Patel actively participates in the youth program of the Swaminarayan Hindu Temple. For several years he attended Sunday afternoon youth meetings in the small converted Veterans of Foreign Wars hall in Glen Ellyn that served as the Swaminarayan temple from 1984 until 2000. He learned Swaminarayan scriptures, practiced playing the *tabla* (drum) with the group that led singing at the meetings, and performed *seva* (service) by cleaning the temple grounds. He engaged in fundraising projects and contributed several weeks of labor toward a new temple building in nearby Bartlett, one of the largest such structures in the United States. When the temple was dedicated in October 2000; several *sadhus*— Hindu monks—came from India for the ceremonies. (Patel is seriously considering becoming a *sadhu,* which would mean renouncing worldly concerns, training for several years in India, and devoting his life to the service of Pramukh Swami, the spiritual leader and *guru* of his branch of Hinduism.) Two college graduates took their first initiation to become *sadhus* during the dedication ceremony. Temple activities involve the entire family. On Sunday evenings, the senior Patels arrive for a meeting of several hundred people who have come for lectures, singing, announcements, and *arti*. Then all go downstairs for a Gujarati vegetarian meal.

About once a month and on special festival days, Lila Narayan drives with her family up to the Rama temple at Lemont. Before they enter, each family member takes off his or her shoes. They walk clockwise around each of the shrines to pay their respects to each deity. In front of the main Rama shrine, they wait for the priest to receive their gift of fruit and flowers, present them before Rama, and then perform *arti*. Narayan's mother is an excellent singer. In fulfillment of a vow she has made to Krishna, she sits before the images of Krishna and Radha and sings devotional songs for half an hour before the family returns home.

Every other weekend, Raj Rajgopal goes by himself to the Venkateswara temple in Aurora. After attending Hindu Student Association meetings at a local university with a friend, he became the leader of a Hindu youth group. Taking *darshan* of Venkateswara in an authentic South Indian temple helps him meet other Hindus and feel a sense of peace. In the

Hindu Students Council members at a Texas university have placed a small metal statue of the Sanskrit word *Aum* on a pile of books in the center of their outdoor meeting circle. The *Aum* syllable is the "universal sound of the Divine, of God" according to ancient Hindu scriptures called the *Vedas,* and is a universal symbol of Hinduism.

summer between his junior and senior year of high school he went with his parents to visit relatives in Andhra Pradesh, where they journeyed to the pilgrimage temple of Venkateswara at Tirupati. This visit made a profound impression on Rajgopal, who vowed that he would start attending the temple in Aurora regularly.

Vasudha and Maya Gopal are sisters whose parents do not participate in many Hindu rituals. The Gopals, more interested in Hindu philosophy, lead a *Gita* study group that meets in the Rama temple. Each week, the sisters listen to their father lecture and lead discussions on verses from the *Gita.* They also attend a Hindu summer camp where the primary focus is on Hindu philosophy. Each of these five friends is forging a religious identity for himself or herself. Together they and others of their generation are creating a new American Hinduism.

Hindu temples usually house images of several deities, but most worshipers acknowledge that all represent aspects of the one underlying sacred reality. Individual Hindus have different understandings and experiences of the images of their gods. Most, however, distinguish between the physical image and the divine essence and power that transcends the physical representation.

Some Indian deities travel to the United States with immigrants, first residing in the home shrines of families and then moving into temple shrines. Each deity has its own distinctive characteristics, markings, legends, dress, and symbols, so that worshipers can recognize them in all settings, including new American temples. No Hindu actively worships all the Hindu deities; each gives primary allegiance to a particular deity or family of them. On the other hand, if an occasion to worship any other Hindu deity presents itself, few will hesitate to do so. This willingness to extend worship is not limited to Hindu deities—some Hindus have images of Christ and the Madonna in their home shrines. The primary deities of Hinduism, however, are Vishnu and Shiva. Each takes on several aspects, names, and symbols, depending upon the location, the needs of the devotees, and the strand of tradition familiar to them. Deities can appear in pairs, male and female. Moreover, each deity is surrounded by a constellation of related gods that appear alongside or are housed in the same temple.

A Proud Hindu

Young American Hindus often have difficulty explaining their beliefs, rituals, and customs to classmates in the United States. When they contrast Hinduism to the religions of their friends, Hinduism appears odd and exotic. If they emphasize the similarities, something vital and distinctive seems to be lost. College student Aditi Banerjee describes her frustration and how she developed pride in her religion.

I discovered that Hindus are an oddity as a child, when other kids would ask me why we wear dots on our heads, though I never did nor did anyone from my family. As I grew older, students would ask if we really worship cows and who exactly are the elephant and monkey gods. In comparative religion classes in high school, after teachers would expound for days on the intricate beliefs of Judaism and Christianity, Hinduism and other Eastern religions were briefly mentioned and skimmed over. On one of the last days of class, we took a trip to the local temple. People oohed and ahhed at the exotic statues, observed with smiles the rituals of *arti* and strange-sounding mantras, regarding it all as objects of amusement rather than devotion. . . .

Such incidents affected me. When questioned, I would present Hinduism stripped of its rich stories and idols, as a monotheistic conception of God. I would stress the similarities between Hinduism and Western religions as much as possible. And inside, I would feel, in some part of my mind, that Hinduism was somehow not as intellectual, not as deep, as advanced, or as modern as Christianity or Judaism. Eventually as I learned more and more about the religion, as I became attuned to the subtle intricacies and ancient wisdom, those insecurities and notions left me. I became a proud Hindu and I didn't feel the need to prove its validity or worth to others. . . .

The best thing we can do is to educate ourselves first about Hinduism and clear away our own misconceptions. After that, we should educate others around us and also, most importantly, our children. With time and a gradual changing of the current mindset, one day soon, Hindus can finally be proud of being Hindu.

Although Hindu scriptures tend to stress the importance of male deities, female deities have a central place in many temples. A goddess, often called simply Amma (mother) or Mahadevi (great goddess) represents both the fertility of creation and tremendous power, or *shakti*. (*Shakti* is also the name given to the Indian program of nuclear testing.) At the elaborate Meenakshi Temple near Houston, Texas, dedicated to one of Shiva's female consorts, Hindus worship the female, active aspect of divinity or the male, passive aspect, depending on which is more important to the individual at the time.

Shiva represents the duality of creation and destruction thought to be part of all existence. A striking image of Shiva depicts this duality through a combination of the genders. One side of the image is female, the other side is clearly male. However, the most common image of Shiva is not in human form; rather it is a simple pillar or stone standing on a base. Some scholars say it is a phallic symbol, but for most worshipers it is an abstract symbol of power.

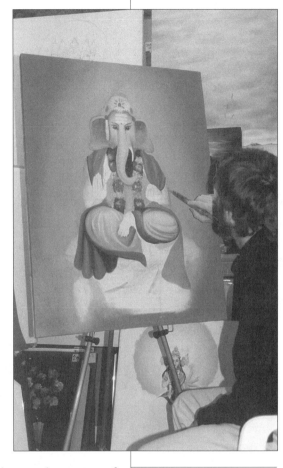

In temples, figures of Shiva in human form sit in a yogic posture of meditation. The god's hair is piled high on top of his head, recalling a story of how the Ganges River, Hinduism's most sacred, tumbled from Shiva's head to provide fertility. Shiva often appears as the cosmic dancer, the Nataraj. Encircled by a garland of flames, the dancing Shiva is caught in midstep with arms flailing and legs moving to mark the incessant beat and passage of time. The serene calmness of his face, though, transcends the ups and downs of chaotic time. Most gods are colorful, but Shiva is deadly white, because he is associated with the dissolution or ending of the world. According to the teachings of *samsara,* the world, and even the gods themselves, are bound up in the process of creation and dissolution.

Because Shiva is so complex, he has many consorts or female part-

American artist David Donnangelo paints an image of Ganesh, also called Ganapati. According to one story, the god Shiva, not knowing Ganesh was the son of Parvati (Shiva's wife), lopped off Ganesh's head. To relieve Parvati's grief, Shiva promised to give Ganesh the head of the next creature he came across. That turned out to be an elephant.

ners that reflect aspects of his personality. Parvati has gentle aspects that balance Shiva's self-denying, reclusive nature by drawing him into the world. She is the ideal wife and mother. Durga and Kali represent two aspects of the darker, destructive side of divine power. Durga carries weapons as she rides a lion or tiger; Kali dances in cremation grounds, wearing skulls and images of death. They signify both the divine force that destroys evil and the impermanent or transitory nature of all things.

Ganesh (also called Ganapati), a son of Shiva and Parvati, is one of the most-loved Hindu deities. He is easily recognized because he has the head of an elephant on a human body. Shiva cut off his son's head in anger but the other gods permitted a remorseful Shiva to restore the boy to life with an elephant head. Ganesh is popular because he overcomes obstacles. People come to his shrine in the temple to pray for good fortune at times of tests, marriage, opening a new business, or any problem or difficulty. Many taxis in India have small pictures of Ganesh and incense sticks on their dashboards—riders welcome any assistance they can get for a safe journey through Indian traffic.

Vishnu has four arms as symbols of his great power. They hold a conch shell, a lotus flower, a discus, and a club. His consort, Lakshmi or Sri, also has four arms, to distribute good fortune and prosperity to her devotees. Vishnu's images portray him as strong, handsome, and pleasant, because he is worshiped as the creator and preserver of the world. One image shows him asleep on the pre-creation ocean just before his awakening creates the universe. Vishnu's concern for the world is thought to be so great that, whenever human life becomes debased and upright people are oppressed, he appears in the world as an avatar (physical manifestation) to save the world from destruction. Lakshmi accompanies him in her role as divine consort. Stories about the avatars are popular, including those about the Buddha, who has been incorporated into Hinduism as an avatar. The two most important avatars are Rama and Krishna, with their consorts Sita and Radha.

Many stories show Krishna defeating evil people and demons. When young Amish Dave visits the Indian stores on Devon Street in Chicago, he buys magazines that tell stories of Krishna in pictures like those of comic books. They recount childhood pranks Krishna played on his parents, his playful relations with Radha and his friends, and his companionship with and advice to the warrior Arjuna during the great war of the *Mahabharata*. Temple images of Krishna show him as a child crawling with a butterball stolen from his mother clutched in his hand, as the wise teacher of the *Bhagavad Gita,* and as a handsome youth playing his flute for girls dancing in a meadow. The ardent love of the young girls for Krishna symbolizes the highest, most intense devotion that a Hindu can feel for a god. Krishna can be worshiped in any of these forms because, as Vishnu, he transcends them all.

The divine and the human are very close in Hinduism. A number of sacred teachers have achieved the status of divinity. Swaminarayan's image appears in the central shrines of Swaminarayan temples, with images of Krishna and Radha in a shrine at the side. One branch of Swaminarayan Hinduism places images of the current *guru,* Pramukh Swami, in the temple. Devotees give offerings and make other gestures of reverence, and the priests perform rituals for all the images.

Priests or *pujaris* in the temples of the major deities are Brahmins, members of the highest-ranking Hindu caste, the group considered purest in terms of religious ritual. India's traditional social system has four large categories—Brahmin (priests), Kshatriya (warriors), Vaishya (merchants), and Shudras (laborers)—divided into hundreds of castes associated with traditional occupations; the caste system, however, is breaking down both in urban India and in the United States. Not all Brahmins are temple priests, even if they know the sacred chants and perform rituals for their family. Nor are all priests Brahmins, especially in the United States. Difficulties in obtaining visas have limited the number of traditionally trained priests in America.

Priesthood is traditionally a hereditary occupation. Young men learn the job in long apprenticeships under their fathers. It is common for U.S. temples to hire *pujaris* from India, because the traditional training is not available in the United States. Priests who speak several Indian languages and English are greatly valued. The *pujaris* also welcome invitations from families to perform special rituals in homes. The larger temples provide housing for the *pujaris* and their families so they can observe the daily schedule of rituals.

Hindu families often claim allegiance to particular *gurus.* The majority of *gurus* are world renouncers who live celibate lives as *sadhus* or *sannyasins.* Many U.S. Hindus regularly visit their *gurus* when they return to India. Each summer *gurus* tour the United States, visiting homes and temples and giving lectures in temples or rented halls. Some temples and Hindu organizations conduct retreats, youth camps, and family conferences to which famous *gurus* are invited as special guests and speakers. These traveling *gurus* are a regular communication link among Hindus in various countries.

The Hindu calendar is full of fasts and feasts. The fasts call for private, personal discipline, but the feasts are times of public celebration. Eating and drinking have great significance in Hinduism, but not all Hindus follow the same regulations. Brahmins are supposed to avoid all types of food thought to be ritually polluting, such as meat, onions, and garlic. Many Hindus are vegetarians, and even those who eat some meat avoid beef, considered the most polluting food, because it involves killing cows, the animals that provide the purest forms of food, milk and butter. In some

A cow receives a sacred mark at the dedication of the Sri Lakshmi Temple in Ashland, Massachusetts. Hindus revere cows for the variety of sustenance they provide: milk, cheese, and butter.

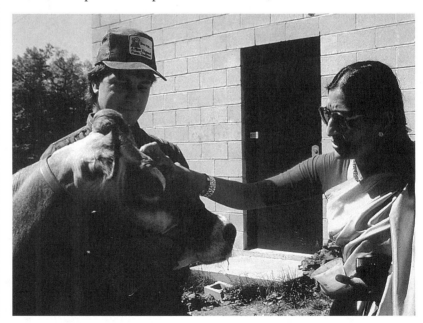

forms of Hinduism, cows are objects of special rituals and respect.

Some Hindus observe particular fast days during which they will eat only certain foods or fast altogether. Kiran Shah, a devout Swaminarayan Hindu, for example, does not eat or drink on two days of each month, as calculated according to the bright and dark phases of a lunar month. On certain special occasions, gifts of elaborately prepared food are displayed before the images in temples and then distributed and eaten in sacred feasts.

Like the Jewish calendar, the Hindu calendar is based on the cycles of the moon. Fast days and feast days fall upon different dates from year to year. In India, people observe many feasts, festivals, and holy days throughout the year, creating a round of sacred time that transcends the ordinary calendar of daily activities. In the United States, Hindus find it necessary to gather for only the most important festivals and to observe them on weekends when people are free from work. On major festival days, many Hindu families try to visit temples even if they have to travel a great distance. Temples in large cities become very crowded, so some festivities must be held in large halls or convention centers.

Diwali, the festival of lights, is an all-India festival that most American Hindus observe in October or November. It is a five-day festival during which lights decorate homes and buildings, because Lakshmi is said to visit each house that is clean and brightly lit. Families try to gather then, for Diwali is a time of new clothes, feasting, exchanging gifts and greeting cards, and parties. It also marks the beginning of a new business year, so accounts are settled. Business people bring their new account books to the temple or to their *guru* to be specially blessed for the new year. Diwali is a happy festival, marking the victory of light over darkness, good over evil.

Festivals honor the birthdays of the most important deities. Rama's is in March or April. Delicacies are eaten in place of regular food, and readings, performances, and interpretations of the *Ramayana* are part of the observance. While other Hindus are celebrating the birth of Rama, followers of Swaminarayan celebrate their leader's birth, which is supposed to have taken place at 10:10 P.M., so the celebration reaches its climax at that most sacred time. Red garments and golden crowns are placed on the image of Swaminarayan, and the finest foods are offered, then distributed to the devotees. The day is spent in chanting the Swaminarayan *mantra*, singing devotional songs, and listening to religious discourses. A small image is placed in a decorated cradle; beginning at the sacred time, and devotees take turns rocking the cradle.

Krishna's birth is celebrated in July or August. The birth is honored at midnight in the temple. Worshipers offer devotion to the child Krishna with singing and gifts, and then eat sweet food all night. The next day is a fast day, followed by a feast in the evening. All temples with images of Krishna and Radha host large celebrations, but this festival is most important for the ISKCON temples, which are dedicated to Krishna.

Navaratri is a nine-day celebration in September and October associated with both the goddess Durga (so it is also called Durga Puja) and the god Rama. Bengali families help organize elaborate celebrations for nine nights, because Durga is very popular in Bengal. Other groups organize readings and performances of the *Ramayana* or other sacred texts. The festival, which includes folk dancing and feasting, ends on the tenth day, marking the defeat and death of the demon king Ravana. The Navaratri celebration in Edison, New Jersey, has become one of America's largest religious annual festivals, with more than 10,000 people attending. A procession makes its way through the streets of Edison. Groups of men, women, and youths perform traditional stick dances in joyous celebration. An evening of music, dance, and drama performances completes the celebration. Young people have said that participating in the public Navaratri celebration with thousands of others makes them proud to be Indian and Hindu. Gradually Hindu festivals are becoming more visible among U.S. holidays.

Making pilgrimages to sacred temples and sites is an important part of Hinduism. When Uma Dwarakanth visits her family in India, she goes for *darshan* at several famous temples. On one trip, she bathed in the Ganges River. Many American Hindu families plan their vacations to include trips to the large temples in the United States. In a combination of sacred devotion and ordinary sightseeing that is common to most pilgrimages, one couple spent a summer vacation driving across the United States, stopping to visit friends and to have *darshan* at the temples of Vishnu and Shiva near

San Antonio, Texas; Meenakshi in Pearland, Texas; Venkateswara in Aurora, Illinois; Rama in Lemont, Illinois; Krishna in New Vrindaban in West Virginia; Venkateswara in Penn Hills, Pennsylvania; Swaminarayan in Edison, New Jersey; and Ganesh in Flushing, New York. The pilgrimage route is different for each family, but a pilgrimage cycle is emerging.

Hindu temples and their supporters are patrons of traditional Indian arts. They hire temple architects who know the sacred scriptures to design U.S. temples, and they import skilled craftsmen from India to do the finishing work on the temple interiors and towers. The arts thrive in the temples. Snehal Mehta is one of many girls who go to their temples each week to learn Indian classical dance. Based on Hindu sacred texts, the dances are designed to be performed in honor of the deities. Temples sponsor performances by famous Indian dancers who are touring the United States.

Dramatic and musical performances by both professionals and ama-

The 19th-century reformer Swaminarayan, worshiped as the manifestation of the highest divinity, wears a gold crown and fine clothing for Diwali, the Indian festival of lights. The gurus of this temple in Queens, New York, are pictured at right. Worshippers offer Gujarati delicacies and an American cake. Later, family and friends will share the offerings.

teurs bring alive incidents from the *Ramayana, Mahabharata,* the *puranas,* and other Hindu religious texts. Members of temple congregations put their talents and knowledge to use in performances that are both cultural and religious expressions. For example, Manisha Krishnamurti was trained as a singer in Madras (now called Chennai) before she married and emigrated to join her husband in New York. Whenever possible, she attends concerts by visiting Indian musicians. Although she no longer performs professionally, she occasionally sings devotional songs for Hindu groups, accompanied by local musicians playing traditional instruments.

Hindu temples and festivals sprouted locally in the United States primarily under the leadership of immigrants who are not religious specialists. They relied on their own initiative, on memory of the ways things were done in India, on instructions from visiting *gurus* and priests, and, more rarely, on *gurus* or priests who also emigrated from India. As the numbers of Hindus and the strength of their religious institutions have increased, some national organizations have emerged.

The Vishwa Hindu Parishad is an organization that maintains informal ties among local and national Hindu groups, temples, and religious leaders. Its goals are to maintain Hindu identity and to spread Hindu teachings in the United States. This organization generally emphasizes the Hindu foundation of Indian culture and society and supports the political goals of the Bharatiya Janata party, a nationalist Hindu political party in India. The annual meetings of the Vishwa Hindu Parishad bring together local Hindu community leaders and religious teachers and preachers from India to address the problems that Hindu individuals, families, and organizations face in America.

In the first few decades after immigration began in 1965, communication among Hindus was very informal, often only a handwritten notice of a religious meeting pinned to the announcement board in an Indian shop. Now each temple and organization has a mailing list for its newsletters and journals. *Hinduism Today,* the newspaper distributed from a Hawaiian ashram, has a circulation of 250,000. Most articles are about Hindu activities in the United States and Canada, but the newspaper also surveys developments in India and in other countries where

Hindus live. A few Hindu organizations support religious programs on local cable-access South Asian television channels. Many of the immigrants have built Internet Websites for Hindu temples and organizations.

As people emigrated from India to many countries during the second half of the 20th century, Hinduism became a "world religion," a designation once reserved for Buddhism, Christianity, Judaism, and Islam. Today immigrants and their children in the United States often talk on the phone or communicate through e-mail with relatives in India and other countries. Many return to India every year or two. Visitors from India, whether relatives of immigrants or traveling religious leaders, are a conservative influence in the United States. Even as Hinduism evolves and adapts to the U.S. environment, these visitors provide reminders of tradition and the Indian way. At the same time, they return to India with insights and experiences gained in the United States, and these gradually influence the way things are done in Hindu institutions in India. Advances in communication are making the world smaller all the time, and as the movement of people creates new forms of Hinduism those variations will find themselves in ever-closer contact with followers of other religious traditions. Nowhere is this development more evident than in the United States of America.

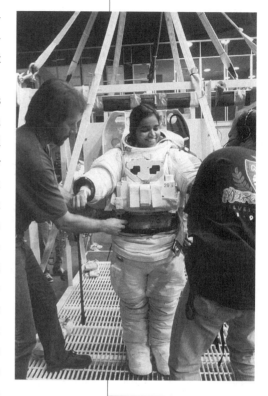

Astronaut Kalpana Chawla immigrated to the United States as part of the "brain drain." The first Asian-Indian woman in space, she traveled 6.5 million miles in 252 orbits of the Earth on her first NASA mission.

Chapter 7

The Sikh Identity

At Camps, Young U.S. Sikhs Cling to Heritage," proclaims the title of a July 1998 *New York Times* front-page article. The story is about the Sikhs, members of a religion that originated 500 years ago in northwestern India and is now part of the religious landscape of the United States. It describes the Sikh community's efforts to pass on its religious heritage to the younger generation growing up in North America. Like other religious communities, Sikhs have learned that summer camps are an effective way to achieve this goal. At camps where young people live, learn, and play, older Sikhs make a concerted effort to immerse the young in the Sikh way of life, to teach them Sikh beliefs and history, and to fill them with pride in the richness of the Sikh background. The *Times* reporter noted that Sikh parents had grown concerned when they realized that "their children could chant rap songs but not Sikh scriptures, could name the Ten Commandments but not the ten Sikh gurus [teachers]," who guided the community in the early phases of its development.

These camps also provide a place where Sikh children can easily make friends with each other—friendships for which they often may have yearned in local schools that have no other Sikh children. "We have kids whose families have become so integrated [into mainstream society] that some of these kids have never had a Sikh friend before coming to camp," said a counselor at a camp in Chambersburg, Pennsylvania. After a ses-

In this 1916 photograph taken in Astoria, Oregon, Rattan Kaur and Bakhshish Singh Dhillon (seated, second and third from left) pose with their children, Kapur, Karm, Kartar, and Budh, and three friends. All of the men were fellow employees at the Hammond Lumber Mill.

113

sion at camp, the young Sikhs return home having learned much more in a group environment than their parents could teach them within their individual families.

The Sikh experience in the United States is now several generations old, as the story of the Dhillon family shows. Kartar Dhillon, born in 1915 in Simi Valley, California, was the first Sikh girl born in the United States. Her father, Bakhshish Singh Dhillon, came from a farming background in the Punjab, a region of northwestern India that was the homeland of the Sikhs. Like many of his generation, he joined the British army while in his late teens. He served in China for 10 years, during which time he had two opportunities to visit California. In 1899 he left the army and emigrated to the United States. Eleven years later he returned to the Punjab, got married, and then came back to the United States, bringing with him his young wife, Rattan Kaur, the first Sikh woman to enter the country. The Dhillons moved around in search of work and finally settled down in California's San Joaquin Valley. They had five children before Bakhshish died in 1926. The mother died in 1932, the year her daughter Kartar graduated from high school. After the death of the Dhillon parents, Kapur Singh, the oldest child, wanted the younger siblings to return to the Punjab, but they refused. They felt California to be home and did not see the point of returning to the Punjab.

Kartar Dhillon married Surat Singh Gill, a Sikh who was a neighbor. He was also a farmer who held a degree in political science from the University of California at Berkeley. They had two daughters: Ayesha, who received a doctoral degree in genetics from Berkeley, and Dildar, with a doctorate in education from the University of San Francisco. They also raised Surat's son, Pritam, from a previous marriage to a British woman Surat had met at Berkeley. Pritam earned a bachelor's degree from Berkeley and is an artist.

Kartar, who has lived and worked in San Francisco since 1943, speaks warmly of her Sikh heritage. She is proud that her parents taught her to read and speak Punjabi, their native language. In turn, she has helped pass the Sikh heritage on to her own descendants. In 1999 her granddaughter, Erika Surat Andersen, completed a 26-minute dramatic film

A band of Hindus on a transpacific liner landing at San Francisco. During the week of February 5 thr hundred and twenty-seven came through the Golden Gate. There are now ten thousand Hindus in Ca fornia. Their first entry was into British Columbia and the Puget Sound country, where a race-war b came quickly kindled and resulted in serious riots. The northern winters, however, turned the Orienta to the south, and they have become an element to be reckoned with in the labor situation of Californ They are, on the whole, inferior workmen. They manifest no interest in the country or its customs; a they differ from the unobtrusive Chinaman by being sullen and uncompromising in adhering to their hab

The Flow from India

The caption of this 1910 newspaper photo ignorantly assumes that these Sikhs arriving in San Francisco are Hindu. Their turbans called attention to them, making them easy targets of racist remarks. Some Americans saw the Sikhs' coming as a "turban tide" that had to be stopped.

called *Turbans*. Set in 1918, the film tells of a Sikh family forced to choose between its own religious customs and social acceptance in a small Oregon town. The film shows Sikh boys being harassed in school because, in keeping with Sikh tradition, they wear their hair long and covered with a turban, a lengthy piece of cloth wound around the head. The Sikh elders decide to cut the children's hair to save them from daily torture and help them win acceptance in their school and community. *Turbans* reveals the difficulty many Sikhs have encountered in trying to live in the United States while remaining true to the roots of their faith.

The history of the Sikhs began with Nanak, a saint and poet, who was born in the Punjab into a family of Hindus, followers of the major religion of India, in 1469. In his late twenties Nanak had a powerful spiritual experience, after which he left his job and other responsibilities of domestic life to travel for 20 years. At the end of his journeys he acquired farmland in the lush plains of the central Punjab and founded a town named Kartarpur (City of God). A group of followers called Sikhs (disciples) joined him with their families in the nurturing environment of the new

The Core Sikh Beliefs

The Guru Granth Sahib, the Sikh sacred book, sings about the majesty of God and how people should live in this God-created world. The opening hymn concerns the nature of the divine truth and order:

> The ancient truth, ageless truth
> Is also, now truth.
> And Nanak says,
> It will always be truth.
> By order
> shapes take shape—
> An order
> that cannot be uttered—
> By order
> creatures live;
> By order
> each finds its status;
> By order
> high and low;
> By written order
> joy or sadness.
> By order
> some are given alms;
> By order
> others ever wander.
> Under the order
> it is all that is;
> Beyond that order,
> nothing.
> Nanak says,
> to understand that order
> Is to say good-bye to
> "I."

A woman at the Sikh Center of Orange County, California reads the Guru Granth Sahib. Sikhs show their reverence for the Guru Granth Sahib by placing the book on a small bed with a canopy over it. Worshipers cover their heads and sit at a lower level than the text.

town. Nanak became Guru Nanak (Nanak the teacher), and the daily routine of community life was built around his spiritual ideals.

Guru Nanak's teachings focused on the unity and uniqueness of God, the creator lord (called Kartar or Patishah or Sahib) of the universe, who governs the world with commands based on the twin principles of justice *(nian)* and grace *(nadar)*. As the creator of the universe, God is the only proper object of human worship. There is absolutely no role for multiple gods or spirits or angels in Guru Nanak's vision of reality.

The universe came into being as the result of divine will. As the creation of God, the world and all the human beings in it are assigned a high degree of holiness, with humans positioned at the top of the order of creation. No matter what their gender or social status, human beings have the unique opportunity to achieve liberation *(mukti),* or release from the cycle of birth, death, and rebirth. One who achieves *mukti* becomes one with God.

Although this liberation comes as a divine gift, humans are expected to prepare themselves to receive it. This preparation includes controlling self-centeredness by developing a relationship with God based on love and fear. Another element of preparation is cultivating a constant remembrance of God's power. Guru Nanak traces the movement toward

Along with Chinese and other immigrant groups, Sikhs built the Pacific & Eastern Railroad in Oregon, hard labor that local people were not very anxious to take up.

liberation through five stages or realms. It starts with the recognition that the universe runs according to a divine plan and that God alone judges our activity. This develops into a realization of the vastness and complexity of the divine creation, and then into humility arising from an understanding of the nature of human existence in this God-created universe. These stages complete the preparation of human beings, who wait to receive divine grace. Once the grace is shown, the humans are raised to the realm of truth, a mystical state that cannot be explained in human language.

Hard work, sharing the fruits of one's labor, and service to humanity are the other Sikh enduring assets in pursuing liberation. The family and community are not a backdrop to an individual's search for liberation; they are a part of the search. Guru Nanak believed that individuals have a duty to work toward the liberation of all. According to him, a successful individual attains liberation for himself or herself as well as assisting in the liberation of everyone around. This is not a choice but a moral command.

Guru Nanak composed more than 400 hymns in Punjabi. He modified the existing writing systems of his time to create *Gurmukhi,* the script of the Sikhs; then gave this new script sacred status and wrote his compositions in it. He saw his hymns as the word of God. Later they formed the core of what became the Guru Granth Sahib, or Sikh scripture, whose name means "Honorable guru in book form." The Guru Granth Sahib is the highest authority within the Sikh community as well as the center of Sikh ritual and ceremonial life. It contains about 3,000 poetic compositions, which are understood to hold the divine message as revealed to early Sikhs.

The communal nature of Guru Nanak's teachings, with their emphasis on shared experience and community life, helped shape the institutional structure of Sikhism that emerged at Kartarpur. Guru Nanak began the practice of reciting three daily prayers: at sunrise, at sunset, and just before going to sleep. He also established a community kitchen where all Sikhs were to eat together in a manner that reflected their belief in human equality. The concept of a community kitchen embodied the Sikhs' rejection of the caste and gender distinctions prevailing in the Hindu society that surrounded them, and it became an enduring Sikh institution. At the time of his death in 1538 or 1539, Guru Nanak appointed one of his followers, Angad, to be his successor. By doing so, Guru Nanak made the office of guru a formal institution. Angad served as guru until his death in 1552.

During the 16th century, the Sikh center moved from Kartarpur to a town that later came to be known by its present name of Amritsar. This name, which means "pool of nectar," refers to a large pool in which a temple called the Darbar Sahib, the holiest Sikh pilgrimage site, stands. The Sikh community founded other towns as well. The locations of these settlements indicate that a group called the Jats, formerly livestock-herding nomads who had begun to become settled farmers in the 12th century, had joined the Sikhs in large numbers. The Jats brought with them a tradition of defying authority that was to shape the next stage of Sikh history.

In the late 16th century much of India was ruled by Akbar, emperor of the Mughals or Moguls, a Muslim people who had conquered the region. Akbar was a liberal believer who permitted a great degree of religious freedom to non-Muslims. When he died in 1605, his son Jahangir succeeded him on the throne. Under Jahangir, administrators in the imperial capital of Delhi and in Lahore, the capital of the province where the Sikhs lived, came to view the Sikhs as a threat. The tension led to the execution of Guru Arjan, the fifth Sikh guru, in 1606.

Under Guru Arjan's successor, Guru Hargobind, the Sikhs responded by formally rejecting Mughal authority. They recognized the guru as not only their spiritual leader but their worldly one as well. The Sikhs were then forced to leave Amritsar. Eventually, driven out of the Punjab plains, they moved to the foothills of the Himalayas. There they established new settlements: Kiratpur (City of Praise) in the 1630s and Anandpur (City of Ecstasy) in the 1660s, in states ruled by Hindu chiefs. An attempt to revive the original community on the plains during the leadership of Guru Tegh Bahadur, the ninth Sikh guru, ended with his execution in Delhi in 1675.

In this hostile political environment, the Sikh belief in God's justice took the form of a special declaration by Guru Gobind Singh, the tenth guru. In 1699, he announced that from then on the Sikh community was to be understood as the Khalsa—"the pure people"—distinct from others in the surrounding world. By insisting on the pure and separate identities of the Sikhs, Guru Gobind Singh gave them a new understanding of their special relationship to God and their mission to establish the Khalsa Raj (Kingdom of the Khalsa), a state where that relationship could flourish.

Guru Gobind Singh introduced a ceremony called *Khande di pahul* (nectar of the double-edged sword). This ceremony involved stirring fresh water with a double-edged sword, symbol of God's power and justice, while reciting over it the compositions of the gurus. The ceremony was thought to transform the water into a holy liquid called nectar. Having taken the nectar, a Sikh became a Singh (lion), expected to follow an expanded version of a code of conduct that had existed in the community since the days of Guru Nanak. The new, expanded code involved following several practices: abstaining from tobacco and carrying or wearing the "five Ks" on one's person. These Ks were *kes* (uncut hair), *kangha* (a comb), *kirpan* (a sword), *karha* (a steel bracelet), and *kachha* (longer than usual shorts). Abstaining from using tobacco and leaving one's hair uncut represented the Sikh belief in the sanctity of the body, a divine temple not to be made unclean. The comb represented the Sikh belief in the importance of keeping the hair clean; in addition, Sikh men adopted a custom of tying their long hair into a knot and covering it with a turban. The remaining three items were associated with war. The sword was to be used to defend the community and pursue justice when needed, the steel bracelet protected the wrist during battle, and the short breeches were seen as effective dress for a warrior.

At the time of his death in 1708, Guru Gobind Singh had discontinued the office of the guru. He declared that the Granth or sacred text would serve as the guru in the future. The personal guru was replaced with the divine word enshrined in Sikh scripture, making the Sikhs literally the people of the book. The Sikh community was collectively assigned the authority to interpret the sacred text.

The vision of establishing the kingdom of the Khalsa fired the Sikh imagination in the 18th century. The Khalsa, or Sikh community at large, saw itself as the army of God, working on the belief that if peaceful means fail to bring justice, it is proper to wage war. Sikhs developed a powerful myth centered on the belief that the land of the Punjab belongs to them, a special gift from the tenth guru. After waging relentless military campaigns all through the 18th century, finally, under the leadership of Ranjit Singh, a great army general and shrewd administrator, they created a powerful kingdom in the Punjab. The Sikhs' understanding of the Khalsa as the pure or special ones, however, did not make them try to convert others to their faith. Even at the peak of their political power they remained a small minority in the Punjab. Their numbers probably never exceeded 10 percent of the total population in the region.

The death of Ranjit Singh in 1839 ushered in a period of instability, and the British, who had ruled India for many years, took control of the Punjab in 1849. After an early phase of painful self-examination and reflection on the fall of their kingdom, the Sikhs began to work closely with their conquerors. The British declared the Sikhs to be a "martial [militant] race" and recruited them into the imperial army and the police, creating opportunities for worldwide travel. Bakhshish Dhillon was just one of many Sikhs who served in and finally settled in a foreign country as a result of his military service for the British.

The coming of the British and the modern institutions they brought to the Punjab stimulated a Sikh revival movement called the Singh Sabha (Society of the Singhs). The movement's leaders labored to make Sikhs aware of what they saw as the correct Sikh doctrines and practices. They used printing technology introduced by the British to publish and distribute documents about Sikh history and literature. In addition, they worked closely with the British administrators, convincing them of the importance of treating Sikhs as a distinct political community.

In 1947, India gained its independence from Britain, and part of its northwestern territory was split off into the independent Muslim nation of Pakistan. This split divided the Punjab between Pakistan and India. During the long negotiations that preceded the division, an independent

The Sikh emblem is made up of three symbols. The circle in the middle is a cooking pot, which represents the sharing of food in a communal kitchen; the two swords at the sides stand for God's power and justice; and the double-edged sword in the center symbolizes God's sovereignty.

Sikh state was often discussed. However, the small size of the Sikh population among the other residents of the Punjab doomed the idea to failure At the time of the partition of the Punjab, the Sikhs left the newly created Muslim state of Pakistan and moved to the Indian Punjab.

In the decades that followed, the Akali Dal, a Sikh political party whose membership requirements and programs have a distinctly religious character, found itself in conflict with the central government of India in Delhi. The party sought to create a state where Sikhs would be in the majority and Punjabi would be the official language. Its efforts resulted in the founding of the present-day Indian state of Punjab. In the 1980s some Sikhs went further, supporting a movement to create an independent nation called Khalistan. This movement led to much violence in the Punjab from which the Sikh community is still recovering.

But while Sikhs in Asia have continued to work out their destiny in their traditional homeland, others have been shaping a different destiny in North America. For some of them, the American dream has come true. One of them was Dalip Singh Saund. Born into a wealthy farming family in the central Punjab in 1899, Saund arrived in San Francisco in 1920. After earning a doctorate in mathematics from the University of California at Berkeley in 1922, he moved to the Imperial Valley in southern California, where a number of Sikhs lived, and settled down to his family profession of farming. There he encountered Marian Kosa, whom he had met on a ship while traveling from London to New York. In 1928, they were married. As an Indian, Saund could not become a U.S. citizen, because a federal law dating from 1790 declared that only white immigrants were eligible for citizenship. Kosa, although American born, had to give up her own citizenship to marry him.

A change in the immigration and citizenship laws in 1946 allowed the Saunds to become citizens, and citizenship opened doors for their participation in civic activities. Saund emerged as a local leader in the Democratic party. In 1952 he was elected judge in Westmoreland Judicial District Court, Imperial County. He served for four years and then was elected to Congress for three consecutive terms, serving from 1957 to 1963. In his autobiography, Saund tells how his constituents asked him, at an election

Dalip Singh Saund
(far right) visits Indian
officials with his wife in
1957, his first year as
California's representative
to Congress.

rally, "Doc, tell us, if you are elected, will you furnish the turbans or will we have to buy them ourselves in order to come into your court?" His answer was: "You know me for a tolerant man. I do not care what a man has on top of his head. All I am interested in is what he's got inside of it."

Saund lived through several phases in the history of Sikhs in America. At the time he began his life in the United States, he could not even become a citizen. By the end of his life, he had not only become a citizen but had taken an active role in government. For early Sikh arrivals, their day-to-day experience in the United States was shaped by how others perceived them and by laws that set limits on what they could do in both public and private life. Yet it was also molded and strengthened by Sikh tradition and belief and by the sense of a community shared among Sikhs.

Chapter 8

Sikhs Come to America

A few Sikh soldiers settled on the Pacific Coast of British Columbia, Canada, during the 1890s. Others followed, choosing to emigrate to Canada because it, like India, was then part of the British empire. Eventually, a number of these Sikhs would move from Canada south to the United States.

Sikhs began to emigrate to the United States at the beginning of the 20th century. By about 1915, approximately 6,000 of them had landed on the West Coast, either directly or by way of Canada. Most came from the Punjab. A few arrived from places like Hong Kong and Shanghai, China, where they had served in the British armed forces. Puna Singh was one of many Sikh soldiers who decided to emigrate while he was in military service. He spent three years in the army, and the stories he heard about America during that time fired his imagination until, at the age of 18, he left for the United States in 1906. Another was Sucha Singh, who in 1924 recalled his reasons for coming to America: "I was born in the Punjabi district of India and served on the police force in Hong Kong, China, for several years. While I was in China several Sikhs returned and reported on the ease with which they could make money in America and so I decided to go." These early Sikh immigrants, both well-traveled soldiers and those who had left their villages for the first time, hailed from small to medium-sized landowning families in the central Punjab. Many of them had left home to make money, expand their holdings, and improve the status of their families in the home villages of the Punjab. For some, temporary emigration to the United States offered a way to gain independence and self-sufficiency. This is how one of them explained why he had left the Punjab: "To make money and then return to the Punjab and farm for myself instead of on the ancestral property."

The Sikh immigrants were concentrated in the California valleys. They found this dry, sunny agricultural region similar to the plains of the Punjab. With their background in farming, they quickly adjusted to their new habitats. Other Sikhs worked in the lumber mills of Oregon or in railroad construction. Their distinctive turbans made them highly recognizable. People referred to them as a "tide of turbans"—or insulted them with terms such as "raghead." One description of the immigrants said, "Always the turban remains, the badge and symbol of their native land, their native customs and religions. Whether repairing tracks on the long stretches of the Northern Pacific railways, feeding logs into the screaming rotary saws of the lumber-mills, picking fruit in the luxuriant orchards or sunny hillsides of California, the twisted turban shows white or brilliant . . . an exotic thing in the western landscape."

The Sikhs' arrival on the West Coast coincided with a period of intense anti-Asian activity and sentiment. White Americans could not imagine that Asians could ever become good citizens of the United States, for they believed that in order to do so the Asians would have to become part of the Euro-American culture—and this they could never do, many believed, because they were racially different.

Racial discrimination showed itself to the Sikhs in several ways, including verbal abuse. Recalled one Sikh in California: "I used to go into Marysville every Saturday. One day a drunk *gora* [white man] came out of a bar and motioned to me saying, 'Come here, slave!' I said I was no slave man. He told me his race ruled India and America, too."

Discrimination also showed itself in the legal hurdles designed to keep Asian immigrants from entering or settling permanently in the United States. In 1913 California passed laws that barred Asians from owning land, and other western states soon enacted similar legislation. The Immigration Act of 1917 prevented people from certain parts of the world, including South Asia, from coming into the United States. It also declared that people from these areas already living in the country could not become citizens, and it forbade them to bring their spouses to the United States from their home countries. For some years, Sikhs continued to arrive in the United States illegally by coming north from Mexico, but this ended with the Great Depression of the 1930s, when economic strains led to a severe job shortage. The following decades were a period of extreme personal hardship for the Sikhs in the United States.

During this period, Stockton, California, emerged as the center of U.S. Sikh life. Some Sikhs had managed to acquire farms in the area and saw Stockton as a good meeting point. It was on a railway line, which allowed other Sikhs who were working as migrant laborers to come into the town on festival days. The first Sikh association in the United States, the Pacific Coast Khalsa Diwan (Assembly of the Khalsa of the Pacific Coast), was registered in Stockton in 1912. Through this association, the Sikhs established the first U.S. *gurdwara*, or Sikh place of worship, in 1915. They collected $3,400 to buy the building and the land it was on. A contemporary account records their feelings of immense gratitude to God to see the Sikh flag in place on the front of the building. Teja Singh,

Punna Singh Cheema was an early Sikh farmer in the area of Yuba City, California. A large number of Sikhs descended from agricultural ancestors and carried on the farming tradition when they arrived in the United States.

an early Sikh traveler, described "the fixing of the post and the unfurling of the flag," which "fulfilled the vision of Sant Attar Singh, a spiritual figure in the Punjab." The event was seen as the planting of Sikh roots in U.S. soil. The *gurdwara* provided a setting for devotional and communal activity. It included a community kitchen to which, as Teja Singh recorded, "some poor white people also came to eat."

The Stockton *gurdwara* was modeled on those of the Punjab. *Gurdwara* literally means "the house of the guru," meaning the Guru Granth Sahib, or Sikh scripture. The person who takes care of the *gurdwara* is called the Granthi, the keeper of the Granth. Normally the Granthi is a man, but there is no rule against a woman taking that role. The Granthi leads services inside the *gurdwara.*

The key area of a *gurdwara* is a spacious room housing the Guru Granth Sahib, which is placed on a small bed with a canopy over it. Here the community gathers to participate in devotional activity that typically includes listening to scriptural recitation, singing hymns with musical accompaniment, and listening to explanations of the meaning of the hymns. Toward the end of the devotional session, Sikhs make a supplication or prayer *(ardas)* in which they recall their sacred and secular history of fighting injustice, seek divine blessings in dealing with their current problems, and reaffirm their vision of a state in which Sikhs shall rule. The service ends when the Granthi reads a hymn from the scripture; the hymn is interpreted as the divine reply to the congregation's supplication. Sikhs call such a gathering a "court" *(divan).*

Because scripture is at the heart of Sikh ritual life, the *gurdwara* often serves as the place where ceremonies are performed. For example, soon after the birth of a child, the family visits the *gurdwara*, offers a prayer for his or her happy and healthy life, and takes "the command" from the Guru Granth Sahib. In this ritual, the Granthi opens the text at random. The hymn that appears in the left-hand top corner of the page is regarded as the divine reply to the supplication. The opening letter of the hymn then becomes the first letter in the newborn child's name.

In Sikh marriage ceremonies, the bride and groom walk around the scripture four times while the Granthi recites a hymn of four stanzas from the text. The ceremony ends with a supplication in which the congregation seeks divine blessings for the new couple's happy married life. When a Sikh dies, the body is cremated. By tradition the ashes are disposed of in a nearby stream or canal and the bones are taken to Kiratpur, a Sikh pilgrimage center in the Punjab hills. The family completes a reading from the Guru Granth Sahib, and relatives and friends gather to pray for peace for the departed soul on a day convenient for all. In addition to these milestones in the lives of the congregation, the main calendar of religious activities at a *gurdwara* includes Sikh festivals such as Vaisakhi in mid-April, Diwali in late November, and some occasions related to the lives of the 10 gurus.

The *gurdwara* at Stockton flourished. Its original wooden building was torn down and a new brick structure erected in 1929. Geographically, the Sikhs of the region were spread across a large area, and some were on the move constantly, looking for seasonal labor, but they all gathered to celebrate religious festivals at Stockton. These assemblies created some semblance of Sikh communal life in California and the neighboring states.

Gurdwaras have always been the places where Sikhs discussed problems facing the community. The Sikhs at Stockton did the same. In the 1910s, Sikhs in California were involved in the activities of the Ghadar party, a revolutionary group based on the West Coast that was committed to driving the British out of India. The Stockton *gurdwara* funded the group's activities. After World War I ended in 1918, however, the Ghadar party faded. The *gurdwara* began providing a haven for roving labor groups and illegal Sikh and Punjabi immigrants arriving over the Mexican border. The *gurdwara* also ran a clubhouse, a facility in Berkeley where Sikh and other Indian students at the university could stay without having to pay rent. Visiting Indian politicians were invited to address gatherings at the *gurdwara,* and the congregation offered financial support for their activities in India.

The fact that the Stockton *gurdwara* remained the only one in the United States until 1948 indicates that the Sikh community did not grow during this period. Instead, the number of Sikhs dwindled and morale sagged as time passed. The festival gatherings lost their original heartiness. In the early 1940s, the ceremonial pattern in the *gurdwara* itself changed. Instead of sitting on the floor in the main hall as in the Punjab, the congregation installed chairs. Worshipers no longer had to take their shoes off or cover their heads if they had cut their hair. These were signs of Americanization, but permission for these changes was duly taken from the religious authorities in Amritsar, the Punjab.

The period that had begun so enthusiastically with the founding of the Stockton *gurdwara* came to a difficult close in the mid-1940s. The number of Sikhs in the country had dropped from more than 6,000 to barely a thousand, mostly in California. Some had died of old age, while others had returned to India. Those who remained in the United States were exhausted by their constant struggle with laws that had been created to discourage their entry into the country and then to thwart their efforts to settle down. Their efforts to seek justice had often failed.

The best known of these efforts went all the way to the U.S. Supreme Court in 1923. Bhagat Singh Thind, a U.S. veteran of World War I, had tried to become a U.S. citizen. He argued that he should be eligible for citizenship on three grounds: he had lawfully entered the United States (via Seattle in 1913); he had served in the U.S. army for six months at Camp Lewis and had received an honorable discharge as an acting sergeant; and, as a Punjabi, he was a member of the Caucasian or white race. After the lower courts rejected his claim, he took his case to the Supreme Court—which also turned him down, denying his claim that Punjabis were Caucasians.

Puna Singh, one of the early immigrants who had gone back to India for a time, was deeply saddened by the outcome of the Thind case, as were many other Sikhs. His daughter later described his reaction: "My father's friend sent him a letter to tell him about the Thind decision and warn him not to try to return to America with his wife. The letter meant my father was no longer a citizen and could not reenter this country." Singh had already been granted U.S. citizenship, but the government soon cancelled it, making Puna Singh, in his own angry words, "a citizen of no country."

Although the state land laws said that immigrants who could not become citizens could likewise not own land, a few Sikhs were able to hold on to their property by bypassing the laws. They placed their holdings in the names of their American-born wives or children, who were U.S. citizens by birth, or in the names of Euro-American neighbors whom they knew well.

The complicated legal situation also created a great deal of agony in people's personal lives. Sikh men were not permitted to bring in wives from the Punjab, leaving them with the dilemma of either staying single or marrying non-Sikhs. Those who married "white" women faced legal obstacles. After the Supreme Court ruling in the Thind case classified people from India as nonwhites, California and some other states began refusing to issue marriage licenses to Indians who wished to marry non-Indians. These states had laws against racial intermarriage, which they interpreted to keep Indian men, now officially declared to be nonwhite, from marrying Euro-American women. Many Sikhs in southern California, however, married Mexican women who worked on their farms. They spent their lives trying to acquire large landholdings that they could not legally own. In the process, they had no time to teach their children the basics of the Sikh tradition.

In 1946 the passage of a law called the Luce-Celler Bill eased the situation somewhat. It allowed only a few new Sikh immigrants into the country—about 5,000 between 1948 and 1965. But immigrants could bring their close relatives to the United States. Perhaps more important, Sikhs could return to the Punjab for visits without fear of being denied reentry to the United States. These changes brought some fresh air into the life of the U.S. Sikh community. New male immigrants arrived with the traditional long hair and turban, encouraging older residents who had cut their hair to grow it out again. Young female immigrants appeared in the traditional Punjabi outfit of loose shirts (the *kamiz*) and baggy trousers (*salvars*). Older Sikh women in the United States, who had stopped wearing such garments years before, now donned them again. As the number of newcomers

Although Bhagat Singh Thind served in the U.S. army, he was denied American citizenship on the basis of his race. This legal position resulted in a great degree of difficulty for Sikhs and other South Asian migrants in the United States.

131

increased, long-time residents slowly began to return to Punjabi customs and eliminate the changes that had been made in *gurdwara* practices.

This rebirth of Punjabi culture did not occur everywhere in the U.S. Sikh community. In El Centro in southern California's Imperial Valley, the number of Sikhs had dwindled to a few hundred by the 1940s. Most were married to Mexican women, and their children were primarily Catholic. Hoping to attract new Sikhs to revitalize their flagging religious life, the Sikhs of El Centro built a new *gurdwara* in 1948. The new wave of Sikh immigrants preferred to settle in the north, however, leaving the small original community in El Centro virtually frozen in time.

The easing of the immigration laws coincided with a rise in the number of Sikh students from India admitted to U.S. universities. An overwhelming majority of these students decided to stay in the United States after completing their studies. The addition of these academically and professionally trained individuals brought an important new element to the Sikh population, which had been overwhelmingly rural in the past. Over the years, the university-trained Sikhs have risen to influential positions in their communities.

Narinder Singh Kapany represents this generation of Sikhs in the United States. In 1951 he left India to seek higher education. He obtained a doctorate in physics from the Imperial College of Science and Technology of the University of London, and then he and his wife, Satinder, arrived in the United States in 1955. After brief stints at the University of Rochester and the Illinois Institute of Technology, the Kapanys eventually settled in Palo Alto, California. There, Narinder Kapany established a multimillion-dollar business in fiber optics and optoelectronics and Satinder Kapany developed a real estate investment business.

The Kapanys' commitment to helping the Sikh community led them in 1967 to establish the Sikh Foundation, which has worked toward bringing Sikh studies into U.S. universities. The Kapanys endowed a chair in Sikh studies at the University of California in Santa Barbara in 1997; it is named after Narinder's mother, Kundan Kaur Kapany. They have also endowed a permanent Sikh art gallery in the Asian Art Museum in San Francisco. In the mid-1990s they helped convince the administrators of the Victoria and Albert Museum in London to organize an exhibition of Sikh art. The exhibit, titled "The Art of the Sikh Kingdoms," was displayed there in 1999 before moving to San Francisco.

A landmark in the overall history of immigration to the United States came in 1965, when Congress passed a new Immigration Act. This act allowed new immigrants from two categories. One classification included immediate family members of people already living in the United States; there was no limit on these numbers. The other category consisted of educated or professionally trained people with the potential to find work in the United States. Up to 20,000 such professionals could enter each year from each Asian country. The new law opened the door for a large second wave of Asian immigrants, including Sikhs from India. Sikh men and women with Indian degrees in medicine, engineering, and other academic subjects, including professionals from both rural and urban backgrounds, arrived in such cities as New York and Chicago. Where they settled depended upon the availability of jobs in their fields, but unlike the earlier immigrants, they were not concentrated on the West Coast.

The new wave of Sikh immigration after 1965 also included families from places other than the Punjab. At the beginning of the 20th century, some Sikhs had settled in East Africa. When political pressures there later forced them to leave, many went to the United States. Another large group of families left Kabul, Afghanistan, when war broke out between that country and the Soviet Union in the late 1970s. Most of these people arrived in the United States with considerable experience in business. They quickly set down roots in large urban centers, such as the greater New York area.

A third wave of Sikh immigration began in the mid-1980s as the result of political upheavals in India. The 1980s saw the movement among Punjabi Sikhs to create the separate state of Khalistan (Land of the Khalsa). The Indian government responded in June 1984 with an attack on the Darbar Sahib ("the honorable court," sometimes called the Golden Temple) in Amritsar, which has been the most sacred Sikh site since its founding in the 1580s. This attack in turn led to the assassination of Indira Gandhi, the prime minister of India, and to riots in the capital city of

Delhi and other Indian cities. Thousands of Sikhs died in the fighting, which began a period of bloodshed in the Punjab.

To control the situation, the Indian government declared martial law in the Punjab. Sikh youths living in villages, many of whom had obtained college educations, were regularly subjected to brutal intimidation. As a result, many of them fled to various Western countries; some as legal immigrants, some illegally. Their arrival added still another element to the American Sikh community.

Sikhs began to arrive in the New York area in the late 1960s. They concentrated in the borough of Queens, home to many recent immigrants from various parts of the world. As the Sikhs' numbers grew, they began to perform communal worship in family houses, with the host family responsible for the food served after the service. At the next stage,

Since establishing the first American *gurdwara* in Stockton, California, in 1915, Sikhs have built more than 100 *gurdwaras* in the United States, including this one in El Sobrante, California. It incorporates architectural styles from Asia, such as the onion dome.

they moved to the basement of the St. Michael's School in Flushing, which they rented each Sunday for a small fee. Then, in 1972, they bought an old church building for $65,000. They renovated the building and made it into the Richmond Hill *gurdwara*, the first to be established in the New York area.

Local Sikhs conducted Sunday prayer meetings at the *gurdwara*. As the Sikh population continued to grow, the *gurdwara*'s activities expanded. Richmond Hill became the center of the East Coast Sikh community. It now offers three services every day and has four full-time caretakers. The leading groups of Sikh devotional singers from the Punjab visit regularly. Saturday is reserved for marriages, and there is hardly a week when some special ceremony is not held. The *gurdwara*'s large community kitchen feeds more than 5,000 men, women, and children on festival

In the Sikh Day parade in New York in 1999, Sikh nationalists carry banners reading "Khalistan," or Country of the Khalsa, an independent Sikh state they would like to see carved out of the Punjab, India, the birthplace of Sikhism.

days. Because of Richmond Hill's location in New York City, Sikh religious leaders and politicians passing through from the Punjab consider it an honor to be invited there. Even Indian Prime Minister Indira Gandhi, although not a Sikh, visited the temple. The Punjab crisis of the 1980s had a significant impact on the activities of the Richmond Hill *gurdwara*, which became the main center of support for the Khalistan movement and encouraged the Punjab to secede from the Indian federation. Sikh leaders from Britain and North America regularly met there to plan their strategies.

The rhythms of ritual life in the Richmond Hill *gurdwara* reflect those of the Punjab. Every care is taken to reproduce Punjabi Sikh religious life, down to the smallest detail. Punjabi is the language used in worship and other *gurdwara* activities. The cot in which the sacred text is placed, the brocade cloth that covers it, and the prayer singers all come from the Punjab. The food cooked in the kitchen is Punjabi. In political terms, this *gurdwara* is a miniature version of Sikh life in the Punjab, with one exception. As many have noted, support for the creation of Khalistan seems to be even stronger in places like Richmond Hill than in the Punjab itself.

Although at first Sikhs were few in number compared to other immigrant and religious groups, they are now a presence throughout the United States. There are about 250,000 of them in this country, with perhaps 100,000 living on each coast. Other concentrations are in the areas around Chicago, Detroit, and Austin, Texas. This large, widespread community is richly diverse in background and education. Its largest segment consists of first-generation immigrants from the Punjab, but the numbers of the second- and third-generation Sikhs are steadily increasing. Sikhs are found in a full range of occupations, from highly trained professional positions to skilled or semiskilled labor.

From a single *gurdwara* in Stockton, California, during the first half of the 20th century, there are now 30 *gurdwaras* in California alone, and the number throughout the United States may well be approaching 100, some built in traditional Sikh architectural style. But beneath the surface of resounding religious activity coming from these impressive structures, 20th-century American Sikhs had yet to define their relationships with the Punjab and mainstream U.S. society.

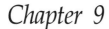

Chapter 9

American Sikhism Evolves

Sikhs in the United States are deeply aware that they live in a country whose culture they did not create. Conflict between the wearing of Sikh symbols and the law of the land reminds them constantly of this reality. Such conflicts date from the first days of immigration— in the early 1910s, a Sikh named Veer Singh was denied citizenship because he "refused to doff his turban" while taking the oath of citizenship. Sikhs were permitted to join the U.S. army with their turbans and fight in World War I, but more recently they have been barred from joining the army on those grounds, although a lawsuit in Chicago is currently testing that prohibition. Similarly, Sikhs have suffered discrimination and have even been dismissed from their jobs for refusing to remove their turbans and wear the caps or hard hats assigned to postal or construction workers.

Sikhs have been a minority all through their history and have faced such problems before. In the United States, Sikhs have sometimes adapted to the needs of the employer; in other cases, they have been quite aggressive in seeking legal remedies for their grievances. In early 1999, for example, a popular Manhattan restaurant called El Quijote paid $10,000 to a Sikh who had been refused service because he would not remove his turban. More importantly, the restaurant changed its sign, which now reads: "Gentlemen must not wear hats, except for religious purposes. Thank you, The Management."

In Washington, D.C., in 1999, Sikhs staged a parade, which started at the Lincoln Memorial. They listened to their leaders' speeches urging them to participate in U.S. politics.

139

Not all such cases have had positive outcomes for the Sikhs. In 1994 the traditional Sikh *kirpan* or short ritual sword became the focus of a court case involving Sikh children in California who were suspended from school after their principal learned that they were wearing *kirpans* under their shirts (California state law bans all knives and other weapons from school property). The American Civil Liberties Union sued the school system for suspending the children, arguing that their right to religious freedom entitled them to wear *kirpans*. A state senator tried to have a law passed that would allow *kirpans* to be worn on school grounds. The law passed the state legislature, but Governor Pete Wilson, claiming that "a knife is a knife" and a threat to public safety, refused to sign it into law.

Some Sikhs agreed with the school district and the governor. One said, "If [the children] don't carry the sword when they go to school, God is not going to be angry with them. I still love my religion. But we have to obey the rules and regulations of the country we are living in." Most Sikhs nationwide, however, disputed this position and viewed the issue in terms of a basic civil right—freedom to follow one's own religion. Editorial writers for the *Oakland Tribune* pointed out that no case of violence ever reported in a U.S. school has involved a *kirpan,* which is typically not much more than three inches long and may have a blunted blade and be sewn into its sheath. As the 21st century dawned, *kirpans* remained banned from schools in California. Elsewhere, the question of wearing them to school remained largely a personal decision for Sikh children. Some do not wear *kirpans* to school; others wear them under their clothing. Further court cases and legislation may bring this issue to light again.

Other Sikh customs also cause problems for Sikh schoolchildren. In 2000, a Sikh father in Riverside, California, told of the anguish his son suffered at school because of his traditional long hair and turban. Other students mocked the boy and, on playgrounds or in washrooms, yanked off his turban. The harassment was so unrelenting and severe that the boy became terrified of going to school. Finally the family decided that the only answer was to cut the boy's hair—the same solution painfully reached by the family in the 1918 film *Turbans.* The boy's father expressed the hope that if young people could be helped to understand the religious significance of long hair for Sikh males, other boys might not have to suffer as his son had done.

Sikh leaders recognize the need to help the U.S. public understand Sikh beliefs and history, and they have adopted various means to accomplish this goal. Some major cities have a Sikh Day parade. Since its beginning in 1988, New York's Vaisakhi parade, which commemorated Guru Gobind Singh's creation of the Khalsa, has become an annual event that brings more than 20,000 Sikhs from all over the East Coast to downtown Manhattan every April. Floats representing facets of Sikh tradition embellish the parade, and with great pride participants explain to non-Sikh passersby the significance of the event and of ceremonies such as communal eating, while inviting them to come and share food.

Gurdwaras work locally with other religious organizations interested in interfaith activities. For instance, the *gurdwara* at Palatine, Illinois, played an enthusiastic part in the 1993 Parliament of World Religions, a global forum that brought thousands of people from different religious traditions together in Chicago on the 100th anniversary of a similar religious gathering in the late 19th century. The *gurdwara* at Rockville, Maryland, represents Sikhs in various organizations and gatherings for interfaith communication. The Sikh community is also working with other ethnic groups to seek solutions to problems they share, such as discrimination, racially motivated violence, and hate crimes.

One of the most ambitious methods the Sikhs have adopted to establish their presence in the United States is to begin teaching Sikh studies and the Punjabi language in U.S. universities. With the support of the Sikh Foundation in Palo Alto, the University of California at Berkeley launched this process in 1977, when W. H. McLeod, a leading Western historian of Sikhism, taught a course on the subject. A major conference

This young Sikh in Oklahoma wears his long hair in a knot on his head, while his father's is wrapped in a turban. Sikhs do not cut their hair because they believe that to do so violates the sanctity of the body.

on Sikh studies that year produced an important volume of essays.

In the late 1980s, community-sponsored programs in Sikh studies began at Columbia University in New York and at the University of Michigan. The University of California at Berkeley began a program in Punjabi in 1992, and the Santa Barbara branch of the university created a professorship in Sikh studies with funding entirely from its own resources in 1997. The endowment that the Kapany family attached to this position adds to its programmatic potential. Conferences on Sikh-related issues have been held at Columbia University, the University of Michigan, and the University of California at Santa Barbara, spurring new scholarly research. In 1997, Columbia started a six-week summer program in Punjab Studies held in Chandigarh, India; that program is now cosponsored by Columbia and the University of California, Santa Barbara. It is intended to help and encourage young scholars interested in Sikh-Punjab studies.

Sikhs hoped that these university-based programs would help spread information about Sikhism among U.S. students, and through them to society at large. Another hope was that the programs would attract U.S. students to the study of Sikhism and establish a tradition of Sikh scholarship outside the Punjab. These things are happening slowly but surely. Fifteen or so scholars in the United States are at present writing doctoral dissertations on Sikh-Punjab subjects. But the Punjab, for all its historic importance, is not the only center of Sikhism attention today. The large-scale migration to the United States has brought new challenges and opportunities for the Sikh community. One challenge is that, for the first time in their history, Sikhs need to draw clearer lines between the religious and cultural elements of their identity. They need to decide what aspects of tradition are cultural, and can be allowed to change, and which aspects belong to their core religious beliefs. The community kitchen, for instance, has been an important institution of Sikh life since the time of Guru Nanak. The fact that the kitchen has traditionally served Punjabi food, however, is a factor of culture. Sikhs have begun discussing whether they can replace Punjabi food with local American food, which is easier to buy and prepare. First-generation immigrants, with memories of life in the Punjab, find such compromises difficult. For Sikhs born and raised in the United States, however, the evolution to the use of American food seems very natural. In their view, the central religious element is the shared preparation and eating of food, not the particular kind of food consumed.

Such decisions, and the way they allow Sikhism to evolve, will significantly affect not only the future of the Sikh community in the United States but the Sikh tradition in general. Another

The community kitchen, called a *langar,* is an integral part of the *gurdwara.* Sikh families bring food and cook it together. To share a meal is part of Sikh devotion and an exercise in charity and service.

example concerns the roles of women and men. In the vision of Guru Nanak, women and men are equals. Sikhs have translated the doctrine of equality into practice in their religious lives. Women play key roles in family worship as well as in devotional practices in the *gurdwara.* Beyond these practices, however, Sikh men leave relatively little space for women. Often, for instance, they do not allow women to have a significant say in managing the *gurdwaras.* In 1989, a group of women sought a place at the head of the Vaisakhi parade in New York City, but the men denied it to them.

The respective roles of men and women, like issues such as the food served in the community kitchen, are generally viewed with more flexibility by U.S.-born Sikhs than by many recent immigrants. The evolution of Sikhism in the United States has begun to open doors for women, and within the community at large there is growing willingness to listen to the voices that argue for gender equality—the equality called for by Sikh scripture and belief. During the 1990s, women were given prime spots in public events such as parades. Traditionally, brides have walked behind grooms when they walked around the Guru Granth Sahib during the marriage ceremonies, but now some young women walk alongside their grooms.

The effect of these changes has reached Amritsar, the center of Sikh life in the Punjab. In 1996, Sikh women from the United States were allowed to participate in the ritual washing of the floor of the Darbar Sahib in Amritsar, which had been a male privilege until this time. Three years later a woman was elected to head the Shriomani Gurdwara Prabandhak Committee, a powerful body that manages Sikh historical shrines. Her presence in this position has brought new awareness of gender concerns within the structure of Sikh authority. The day-to-day life of many U.S. Sikh families, though, is still strongly influenced by Punjabi culture. Male and female roles among U.S. Sikhs are still largely defined by the Punjabi patriarchal social structure, which gives the ultimate power in the family to men. Sikh women typically take all responsibility for cooking, cleaning, and child care, and even now that many Sikh women work full-time outside their homes, they are still expected to carry out these traditional roles. Stress arises in many families when men think that their spouses are not fulfilling their family responsibilities. The tensions sometimes lead to violence and tragedy, as when a Sikh woman in Ventura County, California, was mistreated by her husband and tried to drown herself and her two children; they were rescued. Unfortunately, women who experience such problems often suffer alone and will not consider divorce, out of fear of hurting the family's reputation, a cherished Punjabi cultural value. However, young Sikh women educated in the United States are increasingly aware of and unwilling to accept gender inequality. Some have begun to call for the application of the principle of gender equality in both the religious and the domestic domains of Sikh life.

Young Sikhs growing up in the United States sometimes experience conflict between their parents' expectations, which may be based in traditional values,

A group of Sikhs participates in the Interfaith Festival of Chants in Chicago. Sikhs have shown general openness to participating in interfaith gatherings to introduce themselves to people of other faiths.

Moving to a New Culture

Sadhu Singh Dhami came to Canada in the 1920s as a young boy. In his autobiographical novel Maluka (The Delicate One), *the main character presents the inner conflict a Sikh male faces in having to deal with some of his religion's key beliefs in North America.*

Thus Maluka felt that even if for historical and the current social and political reasons, the long hair and the turban were essential for a Sikh in India, were they of equal significance in Canada?

Maluka could not say yes. . . .

He was fully aware that cutting his hair was not a trivial, nor a purely personal matter. He knew, painfully well, that it would shock his community—the orthodox would mourn the death of a solemn promise!

After much thought and many sleepless nights, Maluka took his decision. Still the inner conflict tortured him. He was haunted by familiar faces with venerable beards. He knew that after listening to his speeches in the *gurdwara* with pride and admiration, the orthodox and the faithful had begun to entertain great hopes of his becoming a persuasive exponent of the Sikh religion. And, therefore, the cruel deception of a renegade would give a fierce edge to their anger, for they would believe, and in grief say loudly, that the apostasy [renunciation] of the educated could spring only from some monstrous corruption or vice.

It was unbearable for him to think that soon the tragic news would reach India, and the reaction of his community in British Columbia would be duplicated in his village with greater disbelief and deeper agony. His mother would be disconsolate; Mata Gujri would be heartbroken.

But Maluka had made up his mind. The vast distance from home, he hoped would make it easier for him to bear the grief of his family and friends. In Canada, in spite of his intimate ties with his community, he had started to grow his roots within himself. And although the affection and appreciation of his people meant much to him, he understood and decided to bear, with stoic resolve, their deception and disappointment, their sorrow and anger.

This young man passes on Sikh heritage by teaching his juniors to sing sacred verses accompanied by the harmonium.

and their desire to assert their own growing independence. Such conflict is a typical feature of U.S. adolescence. The conflict may revolve around education. Sikh parents take great interest in their children's education and try to help them in all possible ways. Yet young people often view this support as a sign of their parents' high expectations for their achievement, and they find this highly stressful. Sikh teenagers are torn between gratitude for what their parents do for them and the need to make space for their own evaluations of who they are and what they may become.

A teenage girl from the *gurdwara* in Palatine, Illinois, near Chicago, expressed the feelings of many adolescent Sikhs in a 1994 article titled "Things That Make You Ask 'Kion?' [Why?]" As she wrote, "We find that [our parents] just don't understand us and vice versa and along with this lack of understanding comes the inability to communicate. Perhaps in our case, this is due not only to the generational gap but it has more to do with the differences in the cultures we were raised in." She goes on to point out that Sikh "traditional" values "still include double standards in the upbringing of Sikh boys and girls." Girls are supposed to be "quiet and shy" and to keep their opinions to themselves, while boys are encouraged to explore the world and develop independence. "Sikh teenagers today are confused," she continues, "and need answers, not lectures or condemnation. They want answers dealing with questions on hair, the opposite sex, peer pressure, and the double standards society holds for girls." She concludes that "perhaps rather than scolding or chastising their children Sikh parents should remember that the process of growing up is difficult in itself and the culture their children belong to is one of two distinct worlds. . . . And above all I am asking that all Sikh parents should deal with their American Sikh teenagers with an understanding that certain dimensions of their familial lives have changed with the change of country and culture."

But as roles and expectations evolve, what will become of the Sikh culture? Parents and Sikh leaders in general are concerned with the need to pass their heritage on to children growing up in the United States. This involves teaching them Sikh beliefs and history. A crucial element is teaching them Punjabi in the Gurmukhi script that Guru Nanak created. In almost all *gurdwaras,* devoted volunteers gather children on Sunday mornings to instruct them in Punjabi and Sikh history. The Sikh summer camps, established for the same purpose, have proven even more effective. The results, however, are not impressive. A large number of American Sikh children possess only an extremely limited or basic knowledge of the Sikh belief system. They do not speak or read Punjabi with any degree of confidence, and their inability to communicate well in the language understandably makes them uninterested in the family religious life as well as *gurdwara* activities: They simply cannot understand.

A Sikh starts his day in Los Angeles with morning prayer. Such prayers are centered on human submission to God.

This results in a real fear among Sikh leaders that the children, lacking a clear understanding of Sikh ways of life, will eventually leave the community. The only solution proposed so far is to direct greater effort toward teaching Punjabi, but little progress seems to have been made.

Ever since Sikhism's founding in the 16th century, Sikhs have been intensely proud of the fact that their literature is written in Punjabi and in the Gurmukhi script; these vessels of communication are close to the core of their sense of identity. Historically, therefore, Sikhs have insisted on the importance of understanding the sacred Sikh writings in their original form, which was the vernacular, or everyday regional language, of the first Sikhs. But familiarity with the writings must go beyond simply reciting the words. These verses are not merely to be chanted; they must be understood, and their contents must be translated into the daily lives of all Sikhs. Now that increasing numbers of Sikhs are being born outside the Punjab, the notion that religion should be expressed in the vernacular may have radical new meanings. For many Sikhs, Punjabi is no longer their vernacular but an exotic and little-understood language. Sikhs may need to accept the Guru Granth Sahib in Punjabi—but using the Roman alphabet, or even translated into English, in place of or in addition to the original version.

Another aspect of ongoing Sikh life in the United States concerns the relationship between U.S. Sikhs and the Punjab. The primary aspect of this relationship has to do with the religious authority in Amritsar. How much control does it have, or should have, over the activities of U.S. *gurdwaras?* On this point the Sikh community in the United States is split. The conservative view is that authority for all aspects of Sikh communal life lies in Amritsar; Sikh leaders there should decide how all *gurdwaras,* including those in the United States, are organized. In this view, Sikh communities in the United States and other parts of the world are satellites of the parent community in the Punjab. Their *gurdwaras* belong to a global hierarchy and must follow the authority in Amritsar on all matters pertaining to Sikh religious life.

On the other side, however, are American Sikhs who perceive themselves as belonging to an independent congregation. They do recognize the authority in Amritsar, whether they see it as symbolic or real. Instead of taking orders from Amritsar, however, they seek to contribute to the decision-making in Amritsar. They hope that by doing so they will help transform Sikhism from a religion based essentially in the Punjab to one with a truly worldwide following.

Relations between U.S. Sikhs and the Punjab also have a political aspect. Large numbers of Sikhs in the United States are first-generation immigrants who still think of the Punjab as their homeland. Their efforts in the 1980s to support the "Sikh struggle for Khalistan," as many of them put it, gave them a great sense of personal satisfaction. But a painful truth became evident upon the collapse of that movement and the takeover in early 1997 of Punjab's state administration by a political party led by Parkash Singh Badal, a Sikh leader who believes in a close relationship with the Indian federal government in Delhi. That truth is simple: Sikhs living in the Punjab are the makers of their own destiny. Sikhs in the United States can support the political hopes and ambitions of the Sikhs there, but they cannot define them. Many immigrants to North America are slowly realizing that the Punjab, with its historic *gurdwaras*, can serve only as their sacred land, not as an instrument of their political will.

Until the end of the 20th century, Sikhs in the United States were busy creating a religious life that was essentially a replica of what they knew in the Punjab. Changes were largely on the surface only. This cannot continue much longer. As the American children of Sikh immigrants grow to maturity, they will move into roles of leadership and will make changes suited to their own needs.

Chronology

1844
The Dial magazine publishes a Buddhist text

1848
First Chinese immigrants arrive in United States

1882
U.S. Congress passes Chinese Exclusion Act

1890s
Sikhs first come to West Coast of North America

1893
World's Parliament of Religions in Chicago includes Buddhist and Hindu representatives

1899
Young Men's Buddhist Association (YMBA) founded in San Francisco

1907–08
Gentlemen's Agreement with Japan limits Japanese immigration

1912
Pacific Khalsa Diwan, first Sikh organization in United States, founded

1913
California alien land act, prohibiting noncitizen landowners, passed

1914
YMBA renamed Buddhist Mission of North America (BMNA); Sikh *gurdwara* at Stockton, California, founded

1917
Immigration Act keeps Asians from entering United States

1924
The U.S. passes laws that exclude Asians from immigrating

1930
Japanese American Citizens League (JACL) founded

1941
Japan bombs U.S. naval fleet at Pearl Harbor, Hawaii

1942
Japanese Americans on West Coast incarcerated

1943
Chinese Exclusion Act repealed; Nisei 442nd Regimental Combat Team formed

1944
BMNA renamed Buddhist Churches of America (BCA); temples open in Chicago

1946
New immigration laws ease restrictions on legal immigration from South Asia

1947
Punjab, Sikh homeland in South Asia, divided between India and Pakistan when India receives its independence

1950–60s
American interest in Zen Buddhism
flourishes

1956
Dalip Singh Saund first Sikh elected
to U. S. Congress

1959
Maharishi Mahesh Yogi, founder of
Transcendental Meditation, visits
United States

1965
Hart-Celler Act opens doors for
Asians to enter United States

1966
The International Society of Krishna
Consciousness (ISKCON) founded
in New York; a Sikh majority state,
with Punjabi as its official language,
created in Punjab

1966–79
First Sri Lankan, Thai, Laotian, and
Cambodian temples open in United
States

1967
Sikh Foundation established in
United States under leadership of
Narinder Singh Kapany

1968
Harbhajan Singh Yogi arrives in
California and begins bringing
Americans of European descent
into Sikh fold

1975
Vietnam War ends; Insight Medita-
tion Society founded by Buddhists in
Barre, Massachusetts

1981
The Federation of Jain Associations
in North America (JAINA) founded

1984
Indian army attacks Sikhism's most
sacred shrine, the Darbar Sahib,
leading American Sikh separatists to
call for an independent state to be
called Khalistan

1984–2000
Large new Hindu temples dedicated
in several U.S. cities

1991
Tricycle: The Buddhist Review
founded

1993
Parliament of the World's Religions
held in Chicago

1999
Buddhist Churches of America celebrates centennial of its founding

2001
Soka University of America is established, with financing from the Buddhist sect Soka Gakkai International

Further Reading

GENERAL READING ON RELIGION IN THE UNITED STATES

Ahlstrom, Sidney. *A Religious History of the American People.* New Haven: Yale University Press, 1972.

Butler, Jon, and Harry S. Stout, eds. *Religion in American History: A Reader.* New York: Oxford University Press, 1997.

Eck, Diana. *A New Religious America.* San Francisco: Harper, 2001.

Gaustad, Edwin. *A Religious History of America.* Rev. ed. San Francisco: Harper & Row, 1990.

———, and Philip L. Barlow. *New Historical Atlas of Religion in America.* New York: Oxford University Press, 2001.

Marty, Martin. *Pilgrims in Their Own Land: 500 Years of Religion in America.* New York: Penguin, 1985.

ASIAN RELIGIONS IN AMERICA

Eck, Diana, ed. *On Common Ground: World Religions in America.* CD-ROM. New York: Columbia University Press, 1997.

Fenton, John Y. *Transplanting Religious Traditions: Asian Indians in America.* New York: Praeger, 1988.

Jackson, Carl T. *The Oriental Religions and American Thought: Nineteenth Century Explorations.* Westport, Conn.: Greenwood Press, 1981.

Jensen, Joan M. *Passage from India: Asian Indian Immigrants in North America.* New Haven: Yale University Press, 1988.

Richardson, E. Allen. *East Comes West: Asian Religions and Cultures in North • America.* New York: Pilgrim, 1985.

Seager, Richard Hughes. *The World's Parliament of Religions: The East/West Encounter, Chicago, 1893.* Bloomington: Indiana University Press, 1995.

Shattuck, Cybelle T. *Dharma in the Golden State.* Santa Barbara, Calif.: Fithi-an Press, 1996.

Tweed, Thomas A., and Stephen Prothero, eds. *Asian Religions in America: A Documentary History.* New York: Oxford University Press, 1999.

BUDDHISTS IN AMERICA

Boucher, Sandy. *Turning the Wheel: American Women Creating the New Bud-dhism.* Boston: Beacon Press, 1993.

Fields, Rick. *How the Swans Came to the Lake: A Narrative History of Bud-dhism in America.* 3rd ed. Boston: Shambhala, 1992.

Morreale, Don, ed. *The Complete Guide to Buddhist America.* Boston: Shambhala, 1998.

Numrich, Paul David. *Old Wisdom in the New World: Americanization in Two Immigrant Theravada Buddhist Temples.* Knoxville: University of Ten-nessee Press, 1996.

Prebish, Charles S. *Luminous Passage: The Practice and Study of Buddhism in America.* Berkeley: University of California Press, 1999.

———, and Kenneth K. Tanaka, eds. *The Faces of Buddhism in America.* Berkeley: University of California Press, 1998.

Prothero, Stephen. *The White Buddhist: The Asian Odyssey of Henry Steel Olcott.* Bloomington: Indiana University Press, 1996.

Seager, Richard Hughes. *Buddhism in America.* New York: Columbia Univer-sity Press, 1999.

Tweed, Thomas A. *The American Encounter with Buddhism, 1844–1912: Victorian Culture and the Limits of Dissent.* Chapel Hill: University of North Carolina Press, 2000.

HINDUS IN AMERICA

Jackson, Carl T. *Vedanta for the West: The Ramakrishna Movement in the United States.* Bloomington: Indiana University Press, 1994.

Williams, Raymond B. *An Introduction to Swaminarayan Hinduism.* New York: Cambridge University Press, 2001.

———. *Religions of Immigrants from India and Pakistan: New Threads in the American Tapestry.* New York: Cambridge University Press, 1988.

———, ed. *A Sacred Thread: Modern Transmission of Hindu Traditions in India and Abroad.* New York: Columbia University Press, 1996.

———, ed., with H. Coward and J. R. Hinnells. *The South Asian Religious Diaspora in Britain, Canada, and the United States.* Albany: State University of New York Press, 2000.

SIKHS IN AMERICA

Barrier, N. Gerald, and V. A. Dusenbery, eds. *The Sikh Diaspora.* Columbia, Mo.: South Asia Books, 1989.

Gibson, Margaret A. *Accommodation Without Assimilation.* Ithaca, N.Y.: Cornell University Press, 1988.

Hawley, John Stratton, and Gurinder Singh Mann, eds. *Studying the Sikhs: Issues for North America.* Albany: State University of New York Press, 1993.

Khalsa, Shanti Kaur. *The History of the Sikh Dharma of the Western Hemisphere.* Española, N.M.: Sikh Dharma Publications, 1995.

La Brack, Bruce. *The Sikhs of Northern California, 1904–1975.* New York: AMS, 1988.

Leonard, Karen. I. *Making Ethnic Choices.* Philadelphia: Temple University Press, 1992.

Mahmood, Cynthia, and Stacy Brady. *The Guru's Gift: An Ethnography Exploring Gender Equality with North American Sikh Women.* Mountain View, Calif.: Mayfield, 2000.

Index

Acknowledgments

Several quotations about Asian Americans are taken from Ronald Takaki's *Strangers from a Different Shore: A History of Asian Americans.* Some quotations about Buddhism in America are taken from Tetsuden Kashima's *Buddhism in America: The Social Organization of an Ethnic Religious Institution,* and Thomas A. Tweed's *The American Encounter with Buddhism, 1844–1912: Victorian Culture and the Limits of Dissent.*

Picture Credits

V. Mokkarala (1999), Abhinaya Dance Company of San Jose, Dancers Mythili Kumar, Rasika Kumar, Ami Buch: 93; Photo by J. Berndt: 51, 52, 147; Boston Public Library: 115; California Historical Society, Ralph H. Cross Collection, FN-23366: 20; Audrey Gottleib/City Lore: 2, 109; Courtesy of The Daily Record, Wooster, Ohio, Photo by Joel Troyer: 80; Courtesy of Wat Dhammaram/Wisa Supanavongs: 60; Courtesy of Kar Dhillon and Erika Andersen: 112; Photo by Dr. Arthur Eisenbuch/Courtesy of David Michael Donnangelo: 103; The Pluralism Project, Harvard University: 10, 47, 59, 106, 116, 141, 143, 144, 146; Courtesy of Hindu Heritage Summer Camp: 94; Courtesy of Hinduism Today: cover, 74, 91 (Photo by Marc Halevi), 96, 100; Courtesy of Dr. and Mrs. R. S. and Aparna Venkatachalam/Hinduism Today: 6, 98; Courtesy of The Hindu Temple of Greater Chicago: 77; Gift of the Akioka Family, Japanese American National Museum (93.29.3): 14; Peter M. Jensen: 134-35; LBJ Library Photo by Yoichi Okamoto: 66; Library of Congress: 19 (LC-USZ62-105248), 24 (FLA 17889), 30 (Detroit Publishing Company Collection, LC-D4-72635), 43 (LC-USZ62-119239), 71 (LC-USZ62-115360), 78 (HABS, CAL, 38-SANFRA,151-2), 123 (LC-USZ62-127491); Courtesy Gurinder Singh Mann: 136, 139; NASA: 111; National Archives and Records Administration: 32, 35 (NWDNS-210-G-A584), 79 (NWDNS-412-DA-10682); National Archives and Records Administration-Pacific Region (San Francisco): 23; Courtesy of the National Japanese American Historical Society: 27; New York Buddhist Church: 38, 39, 41; Paul D. Numrich, Ph.D.: 55, 56; Courtesy of Viraj V. Patel: 83; People of South Asia in America Project: 131; Southern Oregon Historical Society #1603: 117; Copyright 1993 *Tricycle: The Buddhist Review,* Cover design by Frank Olinsky, Painting by Robert Moskowitz, "Hardball," 1993, oil on canvas, 108"x58", Photograph by Ellen Page Wilson: 49; Courtesy of T.S. Sibia, Shields Library, University of California Davis: 127; Holt-Atherton Special Collections, University of the Pacific Libraries: 125; Raymond Williams: 62, 86.

Text Credits

"Malunkya's Questions," p.16: From "The Questions of Malunkya-Putta," in Clarence H. Hamilton, *Buddhism: A Religion of Infinite Compassion* (Indianapolis: Bobbs-Merrill Company, 1952), pp. 54-56; "Strangers from a Different Shore," p.29: From A DIFFERENT MIRROR: A HISTORY OF MULTICULTURAL AMERICA by Ronald Takaki, pp.1, 7. Copyright © 1993 by Ronald Takaki. By permission of Little, Brown and Company (Inc.); "Buddha: More Than a Statue," p.43: From Jack Kerouac, *Wake Up.* Excerpted in *Tricycle: The Buddhist Review* 2, 4 (Summer 1993): 12–17. By permission of John Sampas, Literary Representative, the Estate of Stella Kerouac, and Sterling Lord Literastic Agency. © 1997 the Estate of Jack Kerouac, John Sampas, Literary Representative; "Why We Attend Buddhist Vihara," p.54: From Washington Buddhist Vihara Silver Jubilee Commemoration booklet (1992), p.95; "Sisters and Brothers of America," p.77: *Vivekananda: The Yogas and Other Works,* chosen and with a biography by Swami Nikhilananda, published by the Ramakrishna-Vivekananda Center of New York, 1996 edition, Copyright 1953 by Swami Nikhilananda, Trustee of the Estate of Swami Vivekananda; "Hindu Weddings," p.88: "Hindu Approach to Weddings," http://geocities.com/sheenu06033/approach.htm. Courtesy of Dr. Amrutur V. Srinivasan, Glastonbury, Conn., U.S.A.; "A Proud Hindu," p.102: "Hindu Pride," http://ghen.net/forum. Courtesy Aditi Banerjee, freelance writer, Medford, Mass., U.S.A.; "The Core Sikh Beliefs," p.116: From the Guru Granth Sahib. Trans. Gurinder Singh Mann; "Moving to a New Culture," p.145: From S. S. Dhami, *Maluka: A Novel* (New Delhi: A. Heinemann, 1978).

Gurinder Singh Mann

Gurinder Singh Mann is Kundan Kaur Kapany Professor of Sikh Studies at the University of California, Santa Barbara. He is the author of *The Making of Sikh Scripture* and coeditor (with J. S. Hawley) of *Studying the Sikhs: Issues for North America*. Mann is director of the Columbia–UCSB Summer Program in Punjab Studies at Chandigarh.

Paul David Numrich

Paul David Numrich directed the Buddhist Chicago Project at the University of Illinois at Chicago in 1998–99 and now co-directs the Religion, Immigration and Civil Society in Chicago Project at Loyola University Chicago. His book *Old Wisdom in the New World*, about immigrant Buddhist temples, received the 1997 Distinguished Book Award from the Sociology of Religion Section of the American Sociological Association.

Raymond B. Williams

Raymond B. Williams is professor of religion and director of the Wabash Center for Teaching and Learning in Theology and Religion at Wabash College in Indiana. His books include *Religions of Immigrants from India and Pakistan* and *Christian Pluralism in the United States*. He is the editor of *A Sacred Thread* and *The South Asian Religious Diaspora in Britain, Canada, and the United States*.

Jon Butler

Jon Butler is the William Robertson Coe Professor of American Studies and History and Professor of Religious Studies at Yale University. He is the coauthor, with Harry S. Stout, of *Religion in American History: A Reader*. *Awash in a Sea of Faith: Christianizing the American People* won him the Beveridge Award for the best book on American history in 1990 from the American Historical Association.

Harry S. Stout

Harry S. Stout is the Jonathan Edwards Professor of American Christianity at Yale University. He is the general editor of the Religion in America series for Oxford University Press and coeditor of *New Directions in American Religious History* and *The Dictionary of Christianity in America*. His book *The Divine Dramatist: George Whitefield and the Rise of Modern Evangelicalism* was nominated for a Pulitzer Prize in 1991.

	DATE DUE